BEHIND CLOSED DOORS

HIDDEN CHRONICLES: VOLUME 1

Dr. Nathea Watts Hutchinson

Order this book online at www.trafford.com
or email orders@trafford.com

Most Trafford titles are also available at major online book retailers.

Printed in the United States of America.

ISBN: 978-1-4669-6840-0 (sc)
ISBN: 978-1-4669-6842-4 (hc)
ISBN: 978-1-4669-6841-7 (e)

Library of Congress Control Number: 2012921701

Trafford rev. 11/28/2012

 www.trafford.com

North America & international
toll-free: 1 888 232 4444 (USA & Canada)
phone: 250 383 6864 ♦ fax: 812 355 4082

This book is dedicated to God, who is preeminent in my life. To my four children, Stanley E. Watts (deceased), Shannon R. Figueroa, Jonathan B. Hutchinson, and my baby, Kaysha S. Hutchinson, who motivates me to be all I can be so that they are without excuse and will be all that God created them to be. To my daddy, Ananias Watts Sr., and to my mama, Alice Byrd (deceased).

Mama, thank you for loving and nurturing me to life; it is because of you that I turned out to be the woman that I am. You taught me everything I needed to know about life, people, and God long before I got out of the nest to experience it on my own. While others focused on what was wrong with me, it was you who constantly pointed out the good in me. You were a great teacher and caregiver. I will always love you. I'm looking forward to seeing you again.

Thank you for your support, your encouragement, your patience, and your love covering. Surely, love covers a multitude of sin or faults.

CONTENTS

ACKNOWLEDGMENTS

I would like to acknowledge the Spirit of the Living God, who breathed on me, causing me to come alive thus inspiring me to write this book; my four children, Stanley E. Watts, Shannon R. Figueroa, Jonathan B. Hutchinson, and Kaysha S. Hutchinson; my two granddaughters, Dominga and Mia; my pastor, Mildred Watts, who prayed for me through many tough times; and my brother Ernest Lamar Dunning, who God raised up at such a time as this to take care of me spiritually and mentally. Lamar, I will never forget your labor of love. Finally, I would like to acknowledge my mentors, Bishop Gary L. Hall Sr. (West Jacksonville Church of God in Christ), Bishop Carolyn Boston Love (Truth for Living Ministries of Jacksonville), and John E. Edwards Sr. (Northeast Florida Community Action Agency), whose lives I have marked and do pattern myself after. "Mark the perfect man, and behold the upright: for the end of that man is peace" (Psalm 37:37).

INTRODUCTION

As I drive along the streets of residential neighborhoods, looking at the dim lights from windows and lights seeping under the doors of homes, all sorts of thoughts run through my mind regarding the things that occur behind closed doors. I think to myself, *Love, warmth, and family is what takes place behind closed doors.* I can picture a child sitting on her father's knee after he has worked all day, maybe a single mom going over homework with her child after dinner, a young married couple sitting together after supper, watching a movie, or maybe a grandparent and their dog sitting on the couch, snuggled together for affection and companionship.

In my imagination, love is what happens behind closed doors. However, contrary to what nearly everyone may believe or dare desire to believe, unresolved matters such as loneliness, affairs, child abuse, rape, murders, incest, sibling rivalry, and fear, just to name a few, go on behind closed doors.

Behind Closed Doors is about the person you do not see when you see me. This is a written book of stories—some are told, others are untold—of actual events that happened behind closed doors. This book contains hidden chronicles. I am sure that everyone reading this book has experienced one or more of the issues mentioned of things that come about behind closed doors. This is a nonfictional book; it is based on true-life circumstances and real-life experiences, though the characters are fictional.

It is written for the abusers and for those who were abused. Grief, sorrow, heartaches, and pain cross all cultural barriers. Crisis happens! Things fall apart! Regardless of your race, denomination, sex, or culture, all of us know someone who has been affected, or we ourselves have been affected by some of these subject matters that take place behind closed doors. You may find yourself asking the question, is she talking about me? You may even think to yourself, I know someone who has experienced the things she's writing about, the things that happened behind closed doors.

Some may even be tempted to ask the question, is there a god? If there really is a god, how could he let things like that happen to innocent people? You may even question, where was God when I was being raped?

There are times in the world that you and I live in when good things happen to bad people and awful things happen to good people. The tsunami happened! 9/11 happened! Thousands of innocent lives are shattered each year. Some are by acts of nature. Others are by the hand of evil people, terrorists, arsonists, your next-door neighbors, or sadly enough, members of your own family.

You may feel that the offenders should be punished severely for their wrongdoing or even put to death. Where is justice? you ask. But do you cry for justice when you are the wrongdoer? The reality is that many of us have gotten away with some of the things that we believe others should be punished for. If God would mock iniquity, who would stand?

SADIE

Looking for Love in All the Wrong Places

Sadie was raised in a single-parent home, with six other siblings. Because there was an absence of a father in her life, Sadie began a search for love at an early age. This search would bring about much distress, sadness, and misery. Her quest was to find love in the arms of a man. She felt that she desperately needed to know and experience the love of a man, a father figure.

There is an incident that comes to mind of Sadie that had taken place when she was in elementary school. Her friend, or someone she thought was a friend, had stolen a quarter that was left over from her lunch money. Sadie's mother had instructed her to buy lunch and bring the change back home. Money was scarce in a single-parent home, where the only income was from a welfare check once a month. So the thought of not bringing the change back to her mother was scary. What's more, she was only given the one responsibility and had been unsuccessful at keeping it. Sadie remembered being afraid of disappointing her mother by going home without her change. So she approached the boy that had taken the quarter. He of course denied it. At that moment, Sadie said, with tears in her eyes, "If you love me, I'll let you keep the quarter." The boy's reply was "I do love you, because God says you're supposed to love everybody." Being satisfied with his answer, later that day, she remorsefully told her mother she had lost the quarter. This began the cycle of her looking for love in all the wrong places and being willing to pay a price for it.

Growing up in a single-family home was not easy for Sadie. She had four siblings older than her and two younger ones, so she was a middle child, the knee baby. Her mom loved her very much. Other than a few sibling rivalries and a little bit of jealousy here and there, Sadie had the perfect childhood. It really did not matter whether or not her family had money; the fact that she was raised in a loving family environment was enough for her. Sadie did not lack love, you see. She only lacked the love of a father. Her mother made sure all her needs were met—shelter, food, protection, and most importantly, love. They lived in adequate housing; the neighborhoods may not have been the cleanest in its surroundings, but it had sufficed.

There were times at the end of the month when the food would be low, and as a result, they were hungry at times. Even so, they would never go a day without eating. They would have what project kids called the end-of-the-month meal. The end-of-the-month meal is when you look in the cabinets and refrigerator and put everything you find into one pot. Her grandmother called that meal kill-hungry, which is exactly what it did. It killed their hunger.

Behind closed doors, Sadie felt safe, because her mother trusted in God. As a result, she learned to love and trust the same God her mother loved and trusted.

It wasn't until much later in life that she experienced the pain, loneliness, and uncertainties that happen behind closed doors.

The Arms of a Man

As Sadie grew up, she often dreamed of marriage, being in love, and having children. She dreamed of someone who would love her unconditionally. So she began a pursuit after a perfect life, a perfect relationship, a pursuit for someone to love and for someone to love her back.

At the age of seventeen, Sadie gave her heart and lost her virginity to a boy. She believed with her whole heart that she was in love with him. If there was one thing she ever was sure about, it would be how to love someone, a man. After all, she had spent most of her childhood dreaming about being in love and having a family. Sadie believed that if you loved someone long enough or hard enough, they could not resist you, and in return, they would automatically love you back. How far from the truth! So Sadie loved hard; she loved with everything she had—her spirit, soul, body, time, thoughts, and of course, her money.

Behind closed doors, she gave up her virginity in exchange for love. Needless to say, her heart was broken. Later, she discovered that her boyfriend was not only her lover but also the lover of her best friend as well, and the bed he made love to her in for the first time was the same bed he made love to her best friend in a week after that.

In spite of that, she stayed in the relationship with him. Later on, he started verbally abusing her and rejecting her in front of everyone. But because she loved him, she tolerated the mistreatment. Consequently, in her bedroom at night, Sadie would cry herself to sleep. When you love deep, you hurt even deeper.

From age seventeen until around the age of twenty-five, Sadie experienced several relationships resulting in the same outcome—a broken heart, feelings of rejection, loss of money, and a loss of years that she would never get back again.

Nevertheless, Sadie kept dreaming. She never gave up, even in the worst of situations, circumstances, and horrible outcomes. She continuously dreamed of loving and being loved.

At the age of twenty-six, Sadie was married to a man who loved her very much. Through their union, she conceived and gave birth to four beautiful babies. She called them her greatest gift to the world.

Sadie's husband loved her with his whole heart. *At last*, she thought, *someone to say "I love you" to me and really mean it*. It was true he worshipped the ground she walked on. She was always placed on a pedestal with him. After they were married for about a month, things began to change. How many of you know that the person you meet in the beginning of a relationship is not necessarily the one you end up with? Immediately after saying "I do," he didn't. Before the cock could crow three times, he was having an affair. It hadn't even been a full year into their marriage. The affair devastated her. To Sadie, the only way of surviving it was to be crazy. She wanted to lose her mind, believing that it would nullify the pain. But God spoke to her in her pain. "Sadie, you know you are not crazy, you cannot be, you know too much about me." Therefore, Sadie snapped out of it and remained in her marriage for nine additional years. It wasn't until after he had another affair that she ended her marriage of ten years. All her dreams, ambitions, and goals were dead. *How do you pick up the pieces of life from here?* she wondered.

To cut a long story short, Sadie dreamed another dream, to replace the shattered ones.

Still determined to find love, she suffered more abuse and rejection as she began yet another quest, this time, seeking someone to love, someone to be loved by, and a father for her children.

Conditional Love

After the divorce, Sadie met guys that would say "I love you" to her, but their love was conditional. Conditional love is when two components accept the terms of a proposition. I love you as long as you are giving me sex. I will love you if you promise to keep us a secret. I'll love you if you don't expect too much from this relationship. When the terms of the agreement are not being met, the other party usually moves on but not without taking a piece of you with them. This is carried out with little or no regard to you.

People generally do not verbally express the terms of a condition when you first meet them. They merely say what you want to hear. It is after you have fallen for them that they place stipulations and limitations on what you can expect from them. If you are not careful, we can let the cat out of the bag prematurely by giving them too much information. Most guys listen for what is not being said. When you first meet them, they study you to find out your likes and dislikes. For the most part, they know immediately what you want from the relationship. If it is love and marriage, they know it. Yet they still will not express to you their motives or what they want. In a few instances, they may say, "I want the same things you want." Please understand; just because a person says they want the same things you want, it does not necessarily mean that they want them with you. We, as women, give our heart when he only wants our body, our money, or our connections. He did not ask for your love; neither did he want it. Therefore, we definitely need to find out up front by asking what their expectations from the relationship are or, at the least, state what we want from it. A man once communicated to me that a man usually knows, when he first meets a woman, if she is someone he would think about spending the rest of his life with. After their first encounter, he would make statements like "She is going to be my wife," then he would take the necessary steps to make his dream a reality.

In this story, Sadie did not have a hidden agenda. She was as honest and sincere as could be. She was always willing to give 100 percent and then some. You would think that she would have given up a long time ago or, in the least, be afraid to take a crack at that love thing again. But Sadie never gave up; she wouldn't let anything stop her. She was prepared to do, try, or conform to just about anything. After all, her heartfelt desire was to have the affection of a man, not his money or his house but his love unconditional.

Consequently, when she was alone, Sadie would cry bitter tears of loneliness, pain, and disappointments. These periods in the long run would take years from her life.

Rejection

The next ten years of her life, Sadie went through crucial periods of rejection from men. *What is wrong with me?* she would often ask herself. She started comparing herself to other women. This only added to her low self-esteem issues. *Why doesn't he want me?* she would question herself. *My own daddy didn't think I was a keeper,*

Sadie thought. *He didn't think that I was worth staying around for. If my daddy would have gotten to know me, I'm sure he would have loved me.* Sadie just believed that if she was given a fair chance, she could love anyone into loving her.

Sadie started rejecting herself as time passed. She had become so accustomed to the rejection. By now, she expected people in general not to want her. It was no longer an issue about a man. On her job, she became reluctant to offer her ideas or add input for fear of rejection. She settled into an awful state of mind, which later on resulted in her having deep-rooted insecurities. She had become afraid of people and the looks on their faces. She mumbled while she was talking to others, or she would hold her head down when others were speaking to her.

At this point, it was really hard for anyone to truly love her, because she didn't even love herself. Her own lips would breathe out rejection. It was her new language. For fear of rejection, she settled in horrible relationships with people who did not have her best interest at heart. She was defenseless to whoever rejected her, the one that made her feel unwanted or unloved. In a desperate state, she would seek after their approval and acceptance. But that never happened. She needed people to want her. They didn't.

In relationships, Sadie would not stop at anything to gain the approval of her lover. To have a man that wants you is better than having one that does not. So she would say to herself, "I'll lower my standards. I'll do this. I'll give you that. I'll try anything. You can have it your way. I'll compromise. Just want me, love me. I'll accept almost anything and let everything go." Her lover's actions would say, "I'll take everything you have to give. But I need to let you know that I will disrespect you whenever I want to. Occasionally, it may devastate you. In spite of this, I will not stop doing it. I'll just keep on taking whatever you have to give as long as you are giving it. I still won't love you. I know you will try anything and give everything, but it will never be enough. More than likely, I'll still choose someone other than you. Even though I know the jewel of a woman you are, I won't choose you."

Finally, Sadie

In the worst of situations and circumstances, Sadie yet dreamed of getting married. She is in her forties now, but Sadie finally learned to love and accept herself. Looking back on the lost years and time stolen that could never be recovered, Sadie decided to make the most of what time she had left. She gave her life to God. It had not come to mind until now that everything she needed was in him. God had made provision for anything she could ever need. Imagine that everything she would ever need had already been thought of and prepared for her—a husband, her job, and her work. All her needs were met in God, through Christ Jesus. He would even restore the years that were lost. *I must be something special,* she thought, *if God can see me in my entirety and still love, need, and want me. Unconditionally! I must truly be something special!*

Still desiring a husband, she now knows that it was God who put the desire in her heart, and at an appointed time, it would be God who will bring it to pass. Can you remember being a child and living at home with your parents? How they would go grocery shopping and bring home all kinds of food—healthy foods, snacks, and some junk foods. Our parents would make sure we got a well-balanced meal, which mostly consisted of vegetables, meat, bread, rice, or potatoes. Then they would monitor our intake of the junk food and snacks. Thus, before we could lay a hand on them, we would have to ask permission. They knew that we would choose the junk food and snacks over the well-balanced meal. Eating the junk food and snacks before the main course could ruin your appetite or give you an upset stomach. So it is with relationships. We start off looking for love in all the wrong places, eating the junk food and snacks before the main meal. After that, we are left feeling rejected, with a loss of appetite or an upset stomach. Wrong choices, ungodly allegiances, relationships, and pacts could take us from the main course of our life and lead us to many upsets, disappointments, pains, and trauma. Sometimes we get stuck in places that we never should have been. Then we settle with people in the most awful circumstances and believe it to be the norm. So we stay in bad situations, trying to force things to work that are built on wrong foundations. As a result, we've lost our appetite. The junk food has ruined our desire for the right food.

After the Pain

Most of us are abused mentally, physically, and sexually in families long before we are abused by others. It's just that those stories don't make headlines; they are family secrets. That is what the stories in this book are all about. Sadie's first taste of the bitter pills of rejection came from her father long before she experienced the rejection of a man. She spent most of her years searching for someone to love, need, and want her, to validate her before she came to the realization that God could do more for her than any man she was waiting on could do.

SAM

Extramarital Affairs

Sam is a young man that was raised in a two-parent household. Because both of his parents worked, he lived a quite satisfying life and did not want for many things. All his needs were met and most of his wants. I guess you can say Sam was raised on the right side of the tracks, in a middle-class neighborhood. But it really does not matter what side of the tracks you came from; trouble has a way of seeping through the cracks. Hurts, pain, and betrayal, just to name a few, have a way of finding you. Some may think that because Sam's family did not have any money issues or did not want for material things, they had it good. Financially, they did have it better than the majority of us. But they were not exempt from hardships, disappointments, and the horrible things that happen behind closed doors.

As a boy, Sam often observed his father's infidelity to his mother. His father did not try to keep this a secret from his son—you know, his boy. Back in the day, those were the kinds of things a man taught his boy. There was never a time that his father wasn't disloyal to his mother. It was the norm. Sam grew up thinking that this sort of behavior was all right for a man. He never really thought about what would happen if his mother found out. It didn't really occur to him, the devastation she would suffer when or if she learned of the affairs. Extramarital affairs destroy families and dreams. Their victims live on from generation to generation. Countless lives are shattered.

Sam and Samantha

Do you, Sam Stone, take Samantha Scobee to be your wife—to live together after God's ordinance in the holy estate of matrimony? Will you love her, comfort her, honor, and keep her, in sickness and in health, for richer, for poorer, for better, for worse, in sadness and in joy, to cherish and continually bestow upon her your heart's deepest devotion, forsaking all others, keeping yourself only unto her as long as you both shall live?

I will.

At the age of twenty-five, Sam met and married the love of his life, Samantha. He loved her with everything he had—his money, his emotions, and his words. She completed him. They had all things in common—their dreams and goals for child rearing, financial planning, social, and the status quo. Together they imagined the type of house they would buy. They both fantasized of a house with a white picket fence, about six acres, and a stocked fish pond on the property. Their long-term financial plan was for him and his sons to start a family business. They set goals for their children's college. Their vision for the family was beautiful. Sam did not foresee the day coming that he would be torn apart from his family. He believed in the happily ever after.

Death of a Dream

It wasn't until after he started having extramarital affairs that Sam and Samantha's marriage ended in divorce. All their dreams, goals, and ambitions were gone forever. This definitely was not the way their story was supposed to end. When a marriage dies, so does part of the individuals who were joined together in the union. Dreams die. Goals die. Families that were joined together through this union die. The reason I'm using words like *die* and *death* is because death connotes the end of the life of a person. Death is the permanent ending of something.

When individuals open doors and enter into adulterous relationships, life for many is destroyed. Clearly, we see that behind closed doors, in adulterous relationships, hearts are broken, death occurs, and many innocent people are shattered. The individuals may have chosen to enter into the affair, but they do not choose the consequences. Sam did not stop to think of how this would affect his family. He didn't consider the people he would be hurting or how the impact of it would affect him and the future of his children. Perhaps he assumed that because his father had gotten away with it for all those years, he would get away with it too. Because after all, everything he learned about being a man, he had learned it from his father. Needless to say, everyone was hurt deeply by the affair, including Sam. His wrong choices and behavior affected everybody involved. Poor choices today will cost me tomorrow.

The foundation an extramarital affair is built on is selfishness, self-gratification, lust, and greed. Most of the men that become caught up in extramarital affairs have beautiful wives at home. It is not all the time a situation where the wife ignores her spouse's needs or lets herself go after the kids are born. The majority of the men who have had an extramarital affair, if asked, will tell you that they have a good wife, a woman who would do anything for them. But they paint a bad picture of their wives to other women. Saying things like "She never has time for me anymore" or "I don't feel significant, the children are more important to her than I am. I did love her when I married her, but I'm just not in love with her anymore. I'm just there for my children." Here again, most of them are just saying these things; they have no intention of leaving their wives. They will stay with her as long as she will have them, even after the affair is out in the open.

Sam knew what he had in Samantha. Even after the first affair he had, she took him back and was willing to do whatever it would take to make their marriage work.

Betrayal

Here we see an innocent young man that grew up watching his father be disloyal to his mother in an adulterous relationship throughout his childhood. His only example of what a man does and how a man treats his wife came from his father.

Sam lost his dream, the American dream, the wife, the children, and the family. He did not learn how to love and cherish his wife from his father. Instead, he learned how to betray her. When he said "I will," he didn't know that he was saying "I will love you, I will comfort you, I will honor and keep you, in sickness and in health, for richer, for poorer, for better, for worse, in sadness and in joy. I will cherish you. I will forsake all others and keep myself for you only as long as we both shall live."

He gazed at his bride and saw a great pain in her eyes that he was to blame for. Sam embraced her and loved her with his whole heart. The pain that Sam saw in Samantha's eyes was the same pain that his children observed in their mother's eyes. Sam cried out, "How come I caused so much pain for the people that I love the most?" At that moment, he vowed a vow, saying, "If I ever win Samantha back, I will never hurt her like this again. I'm the man that won her heart. I'm the man that vowed to her before God. I'm the man who is responsible for the pain she's feeling right now. I am the man."

THE SWANSONS

Bereavement

The Swanson's are everyday people like you and I. Unfortunately, their loved one was killed in a violent crime involving the police. His death was sudden and unanticipated. He had come home on temporary medical leave from the USMC three months earlier. Their son was twenty-two years old at the time. Nobody would have ever expected his life to end so tragically and at such a young age. Everyone was totally taken off guard. His family was not prepared for the critical changes they now had to face, changes that would alter their lives forever. But how can a person prepare for something like that? We have each and every one of us, heard stories of others who had lost loved ones through illnesses, car accidents, natural disasters, and acts of violent crimes. But you, by no means, think your family would be the sufferers of something so traumatic. I am sure you have heard the devastating stories of children being lured away from their ark of safety, of their parents covering, and being brutally murdered. These types of stories bring communities, cultures, and our government together. We rally around the family that is hurting. We cry with them, join searches with them, light candles for them, and give offerings to them to support them in their losses. All of us are the victims, regardless of color, creed, or culture. It may be their family this time, but it could be yours or our next-door neighbors next time. Death brought on by murder affects the living and the dead. Death by means of murder affects everyone.

Behind closed doors, the Swanson's struggled to pick up the pieces from their fragmented lives. He was their son, their brother; he was their grandson and their uncle, their nephew, their cousin. He was their loved one. Now, they were deprived of his presence, robbed of his offspring. They were denied the ability to watch him grow and mature. Now, they hear and hold on to every word he ever said. They rehearse them over and over in their mind. In their mind's eye, they see all his gestures. They remember his smile and his tears. They long for him. They choose not to talk about their individual grief in view of the fact that everyone is suffering so much pain. To not openly express the pain was their way of covering each other. So each person coped with it in their own way. Everybody suffered alone.

SW's Story

The Swanson's son, aged twenty-two at the time of his death, was brought up in a loving family environment. Throughout his primary years, he played Pop Warner football and baseball. Later, he played basketball for the local high school. At the age of five, he was given a test to determine enrollment in the gifted program, which would be carried out throughout his academic years.

SW had been trained in the church since the age of five. The values he learned all through his training were God first, family next, then others. When SW started going through the puberty crisis in his early teens, he set out to try and fit in. Feeling awkward and out of place, SW believed that if he blended in, he wouldn't undergo the blunt discomfort that he was experiencing while going through peer pressure. He was trying to live godly in a world, a teenager's world, where Christianity was not very popular.

In a teenager's world, disobeying and dishonoring those who have authority over you is more popular than obeying and honoring them. So he disguised himself to fit in as a result. He wanted to be accepted. He walked like them. He talked like them, but he was not like them; it was all a facade. Shortly after that, SW began getting into trouble in his late teens and was expelled from high school during his senior year. Consequently, it left him brokenhearted and angry. Still, he looked for an alternate path to reach his goals.

SW enrolled in a high school completion program at the local community college to earn the credits he needed in order to get his high school diploma. After receiving his high school diploma, he enlisted in the USMC. On October 10, 2005, he was sworn into the USMC. As an active USMC, SW underwent some emotional and psychological anxieties. Because he had never been away from home before and he was in love with his girlfriend, he experienced separation anxieties. The separation caused him to lose heart. From time to time, he became depressed.

He was being trained to kill. He was taught to forget everything he had been taught prior to joining the Marine Corps. USMC is all that matters. Forget everything else! It was traumatic for him. On August 31, 2005, SW was separated from active duty to temporarily retired status because of a disability. He had served one year and three months in the USMC as an Individual Material Readiness List (IMRL) asset manager and separated with an honorable discharge.

On Saturday, October 6, 2007, SW was brutally shot three times by the Jacksonville Sheriff's Office. He was shot twice in the back, followed by a close-up in his chest area. The story, as told by the media, was that he was involved in a home invasion at his girlfriend's father's home. He was accused of breaking into the house, stealing a firearm, and threatening to harm the father before leaving. The media and the JSO team caused him to look like a horrible criminal, a person with a history of violence, in order to justify shooting an unarmed man. But he was not the criminal that they wanted others to see him as. Painting the picture of him as a criminal would cause the public to think that JSO was doing a great job in the community by getting the thugs and lawbreakers off the street. Yes, he did undergo some emotional problems. But who hasn't? Yes, he did have struggles and made some unwise choices. But haven't we all? He did not deserve to be treated like a criminal and shot down like an animal because of it. One of the officers involved acted as if he had done God and society a favor by taking him off the streets. He showed no remorse at all. He did admit that he could have or even should have carried out some things differently. After that, he said the opportunity presented itself, so he took the shot.

October 15, 2007, SW died at Shands Jacksonville Medical Center.

A hearing was held for the two families, the Swanson's and the JSO. The JSO is a family, and in families, we are taught to cover for each other. Families stick together no matter what. They stand up for each other. A family will cover for each other, regardless. Remember your home training; whatever goes on in this house or family stays in this house or family. Always do your utmost to keep the family beyond reproach, even if it brings about hurt, harm, or abuse to another family. Families are to stick together as one and to speak the same language. This is exactly what JSO did to get a verdict of justifiable. They determined that with more training in selected areas, the officers involved could improve their general execution and perhaps conduct things differently if given the same chance. The JSO family agreed with the ruling. Thus, if a man's own conscience doesn't condemn him, neither can anyone. So there you have it—justifiable.

Mrs. Swanson is a member of a family too. Following the death of her son, Mrs. Swanson's job was to protect and cover her family—SW's siblings, his grandparents, his aunts, his uncles, and his cousins.

If she would have fallen apart, it would have shattered her entire family. They would not have made it because of their concern for her. Thus, she assumed her position. Thinking back, she brought to mind an old episode of Scooby Doo. Scooby was saying to Shaggy, "I'll protect you, who will protect me?"

The Way We Were

After losing a loved one, many families do not pull through. They find it hard to pick up the pieces or go back to life the way it was before the death occurred. Sadly, some marriages end in divorce after the death of a child. They place the blame on each other. In some cases, parents and the surviving siblings tend to fight more. In other cases, surviving siblings wonder if their parents wished it had been them who died rather than the one who actually died. Some siblings even wish it would have been them. The Swansons were no different. They experienced great depression, periods of rage, and loss.

They longed for life the way it was before the tragedy took place. They were a close-knit family, an all-American family if you will. They spent hours of family time on vacations, fishing, beaches, travelling, and much more. They ate their family dinners together, watched movies together, played games together. But now they were suffering together, and lastly, they began to withdraw from each other. The holidays were the most memorable. People admired them from afar. Trauma recovery is possible.

A Mother's Memories

Mrs. Swanson recalled a time that she could not wait for the night to end. She had been in labor with her son for twenty-four hours. She was definitely ready for him to get out of her! She was ready to see her baby for the first time, ready to hold him for the first time. Then it happened! Almost immediately after giving birth, the pain was over and the joys began.

Mrs. Swanson remembered the first time she held SW and the first time she kissed him. She remembered the first time she heard his voice crying and her first time wiping his tears. Mrs. Swanson remembered her first time feeding SW and his first bowel movement. She remembered the first time SW smiled at her and when he got his first tooth. She recalled the first time she heard him babble and his first words "da-da." She remembered SW's first steps and his first fall. Mrs. Swanson remembered his first birthday, his first Christmas, and his first day of school.

On the day of her son's death, Mrs. Swanson realized that she did not want that night to come to an end. The night ending, to her, meant she would wake up to another day without her child. How devastating! SW's days ended yesterday. He did not come into this day. So no, she did not want that night to end. Unfortunately, the night had to end. The next morning, she arose to the first day from the time when she gave birth to her son to life without him. A part of her had died too. In an attempt to conceal her pain, she still could not help but wonder how she looked through the eyes of others. Could they look right through her and see the pain that she was concealing? Did they notice how she was walking or talking? She imagined it was obvious to everyone, whether they knew her or not.

How could this be? The child that lived inside me for nine months, kicking me, scratching me—my first baby—gone. Has this truly happened? Is this a dream or a reality? Is it normal for a mother to bury her child? This is not how the story was supposed to end, she thought to herself.

Now engulfed in pain, she had a new list of first-time memories to bear. SW's first birthday after his death, followed by the first Thanksgiving, then the first Christmas, lastly the first anniversary of his death. What terrible pain it was for her. But for the sake of her other children, Mrs. Swanson knew that she had to live on. She thought within herself, *I must be strong for them. They need me now.*

It was Mrs. Swanson's choice to forgive the officers involved in the shooting and the JSO family for the pain that was inflicted on her family. "I would not wish on anyone's family the thing that happened to mine." She refused to let bitterness or unforgivingness make its way into her heart. Her rationale was this: refusing to forgive would mean she and SW died. SW ceased to live, and she ceased to love. "I must live on for the benefit of those watching and for my children," she declared. "I must live on." Mrs. Swanson went from "I can't wait for this night to end" to not wanting the night to end. Now in the middle of the night, she grieved for her son, remembering the last time she saw him alive, the last time she talked to him, his last words, and his last tears, the last time she told him that she loved him. She held on to every word he ever said to her, every gesture he ever made, and every smile.

Today, Mrs. Swanson does not seek personal revenge. All she wants is justice and the recovery of her son's name. The only thing a man has is his name. His name carried meaning to God and to his family.

SMITH VERSUS SMITH

The Empty Nesters

Empty-nest syndrome is the name given to a psychological condition that can affect parents around the time their children leave home. It is not a term you'll find in many medical books. However, it is normal for parents to have feelings of sadness and loss when their children fly the coop. It is normal to weep now and again.

Let's take a look behind the closed door of an empty nester. It is early fall. The leaves are slowly changing colors, and other signs of fall are coming into view. Sade, the Smith's youngest daughter is in her room, preparing to leave for college. She is so excited and so afraid at the same time. Becoming a young adult and leaving the warm, secure environment that she has known all her life is a major change for her. Sade had never been away from home for more than one week. She wept silently in her room as she packed her things. She did not want her parents to know her fears or to see her crying; this would bring more stress on them and cause the transition to be even more difficult for everyone.

Sade could not help but wonder, *Will I still have a bedroom if I decide I don't like it? What if I can't handle it and want to come back home?* She remembered her older siblings that left the nest before her, how, immediately following their departure, their bedroom was changed into an office or a den. *Can I come back home? Will my parents throw all my childhood toys and memories away the minute I step out the door? What about my favorite blanket and my favorite cup?* Sade wept. She was trying to hold on to her childhood and be an adult at the same time.

My parents are older now, and they need me, she thought. *How will my parents fair without me? Are they going to be all right?* As she continued gathering her things together, Sade could hear her mother's voice ringing out from the kitchen. Her mother has a beautiful voice, and Sade just loved hearing her sing.

"In my heart, you will always be forever young, forever young, forever young." Mrs. Smith let the words of Rod Stewart's song ring from her lips, as she puts away the dishes. *The youngest child going off to college in a few short days*, she thought to herself. *I'm so excited!* She felt the joys of accomplishment. After twenty-six years of child rearing, her work was finally done. *I have waited a long time for this moment to come. What will I do with myself?* She reasoned within herself. "I'll redecorate. I'll work on my weight loss. Maybe I'll return to school. It is finished!" she exclaimed. Her emotions were overwhelming. She didn't know whether to laugh or cry, so she did both. However, she did not want Sade to see her crying. *This was the time for Sade to find her feet as an adult and not worry about me*, she thought to herself. *I must be courageous for her.* Besides that, Mrs. Smith had told everyone that this would be the time of her life, the moment she had been waiting for. She declared to everybody that she would not cry. Little did she know that the closer it came for Sade to leave, the more she would cry. She was afraid for her daughter being all alone in another city without the love and protection from her parents. *Who would be there for her if she got sick? What if she gets homesick? Will she remember not to talk to strangers? Will someone take advantage of her being naive and exploit her? Did I instill enough in her during the eighteen years of her life for her to survive in the world without us being there? Will Sade be able to survive without me? How can I let her go and not be afraid for her?* Mrs. Smith wept silently. She felt like her effective life with Sade had ended.

Just as she was finishing up the dishes, she heard a roar from the leaves blower coming from the front lawn. Her husband was busy with yard work. She couldn't help but wonder if he was experiencing any of the anxieties that she was experiencing.

He whistled gallantly as he thought of all the things he could do now that the last child was leaving the nest. He pondered the idea of buying a boat or maybe a motorcycle. He thought of all the money he could be saving. Mr. Smith did not anticipate or expect to experience grief, despair, or the sense of regret over the things he had not done with his daughter and the time he had not spent with her. He had provided for his family well financially but not emotionally or with his presence being there physically. When Sade needed her father, he was out making ends meet, you know, bringing home the bacon. Suddenly his baby girl was not a baby anymore; maybe she didn't even need him anymore. His eyes fought back the tears. *What will she remember about me?* he wondered to himself. *Will she remember me being away at work most of her life? Will she remember hearing her mother's voice, reminding me that Sade needs her father's love and affection now?* Feelings of loss, despair, and deep regret besieged him now. He understood much too late that the most important ages and stages of her life he had missed, and he would never be able to recapture them again. Without a doubt, he had done his best based on the traditions and the culture he lived in. Mr. Smith had stuck it out. He vowed to be the husband of one wife and to remain married until all their kids were grown and gone. He had done more than most fathers did just by sticking it out. Mr. Smith could poke his chest out and be proud for that alone. But at the moment, he didn't feel too proud. His pain was deep, and being the man that he was, he concealed his pain as a way of protecting his wife and daughter.

My Life Back—
Adjusting and Learning To Live All Over Again

> Wholly unprepared, we embark upon the second half of life, we take the step into the afternoon of life; worse still we take this step with the false assumption that our truths and ideals will serve as before. But we cannot live the afternoon of life according to the program of life's morning—for what was great in the morning will be little at evening, and what in the morning was true will at evening have become a lie. (Carl Jung)

Now that Sade had left, the Smiths were embarking on new changes. The theories and beliefs they thought to be true, they were no longer sure of, and what they thought was most important wasn't that important anymore. It was a confusing time for them. What they did not realize was that they were beginning to emerge into a midlife transition. Everyone between the ages of forty and sixty begin to experience both physical and psychological changes. All midlife transitions are not midlife crises, but they do bring about major changes in our lives. A midlife transition is more than physical changes; it is the reordering of priorities and values. When a man or woman is at the age of life where their kids are leaving home, they are usually experiencing other major changes as well. These changes include, but are not limited to, menopause for the woman, midlife crisis for the man, and the care for elderly parents. Some adapt well, while others find the changes distressing. Depression is common during these changes.

Sadly, many marriages end in divorce after their children leave the nest. This is usually a challenging time for them. During the child-rearing years, they lose their individualities and fall into routines and roles. He is given to the man's duties, while she is given to the woman's duties, and the marriage duties are placed on hold.

Learning to live all over again for the Smiths wasn't easy. It involved them getting to know each other again. The Smiths were rediscovering each other. For the first time in a very long time, they began to notice each other again. This was odd. With the children no longer there, they became a little overwhelmed by too much togetherness. The children were fillers for the odd moments, when they ran out of things to say to each other. If the children were home, they could turn their attention to them. *Nothing will ever be the same for us again*, they thought to themselves. *Will this be a strain on our marriage? What does this mean for our marriage? Can we cope with the sudden changes that we are facing?*

Mrs. Smith gazed at her husband from across the room; he still looked good to her, although he had gained a midriff. He was still as fine as always. Any woman would be delighted to have a man like him standing next to her.

There were countless times that they were out together in the mall or maybe at a park that she would notice women fighting for the attention of her man. But when she gave them a look of her own, they would turn their heads or walk away. *How long can I keep the badgers away from him?* She would wonder. *Can I compete?*

I seem to have lost myself in the child-rearing process. Who am I? What are my likes and dislikes? She began feeling as though her useful years were over. She constantly gazed at herself in the mirror and wondered, *Is there anything I can do to stop the aging process or at least slow it down? I have got to get my life back, recreate myself.* Then she took another long look at her husband who was going through the aging process himself. It was as though she was looking at him for the first time. *What are his likes and dislikes?* She began to question. She could not remember the last time they kissed passionately or held hands. *I can't remember the last time I told him that I love him or that I appreciate him. It seems as though we are strangers, two people meeting for the very first time.* In all the awkwardness she was feeling at that moment, Mrs. Smith knew she had to become reacquainted with her man, or she might lose him. *By no circumstances am I willing to let that happen.* So there you have it, Mrs. Smith experiencing empty-nest syndrome, premenopausal symptoms, and the anxiety of losing her husband. She found herself right smack in the middle of a midlife crisis. In the course of it all, Mrs. Smith gathered up the strength to fight. Giving up was not an option. *I must fight through this crisis.*

These types of changes are bound to happen. Each and every one of us who lives long enough will experience midlife crisis. Her crisis was to be expected. There were women before her that had gone through it; there would be women after her to go through it. Besides that, there are millions of women going through it right now. *What did the women before me do about it? How did they handle it?* she wondered. *What are the women who are going through it right now doing about it? What are the statistics for staying married during and after menopause? What are the statistics for finding love again after the children have moved out?* Her only consolation came in knowing she was not the only one experiencing these types of changes. Thus, she penned her questions and would later follow them up by searching out the answers.

Mr. Smith, on the other hand, was going through a midlife crisis of his own. He had heard stories from all his buddies about how they felt going through their midlife crisis. A number of them said that they did not feel appreciated by their wives anymore. One or two spoke about feelings of insignificance in their relationships with their wives and included that they stayed married because of the children. Yet others had left their wives for younger women. Mr. Smith thought of the many opportunities he had to have an affair or even run out on his wife. But deep inside, Mr. Smith knew that even if he had an affair, he would never leave his wife. He was willing to stay with her for as long as she would have him. *She is the mother of my two children, my baby mama. Of course, she has gained weight and aged over the years. But so have I.* Mrs. Smith was still fine, and any man would gladly pick her up at her current age. He too witnessed, out of his own eyes, young and older men admiring her; when his friends thought he wasn't looking, they eyed her.

Mr. Smith did imagine that an ideal situation for him would be if he could get a pretty young thing and keep his wife too. *Having my cake and eating it too! A younger woman will help me with my ego and keep me on my toes. She would also cost me money, the respect of my children, and the loss of my wife. Is it worth it?* he wondered to himself. *Is it worth it?*

Mr. Smith was beginning to have a greater understanding of the changes he had been experiencing for the last six months. *Over the years, I have changed and grown,* he thought to himself. Change is permanent. Nothing can stop it. Everything has its own season. Some people dread change, others refuse to accept it. He had watched his friends make complete idiots out of themselves during their times of transitions, going after the younger women, trying to physically compete with the younger guys, buying sports cars and motorcycles. Some of them dreaded it, while others refused to accept it. As a result, their refusal to accept the changes simply led them to divorce, depression, and frustration.

MARIA

Maria is a forty-six-year-old single woman. She has never been married. But she has a twenty-one-year-old son, who is currently serving his country in the United States Marines. Maria and her son's father met when she was eighteen years old. They then became a couple, and four years after that, Maria got pregnant and gave birth to their son. Shortly after the birth of her son, the couple split up for good. Actually, Maria had outgrown him and their relationship. Besides that, he had been physically and mentally abusive to her. Not to mention, she had met someone else too. Even though the guy she met was currently living with his girlfriend, Maria fell in love with him. I guess maybe it was the excitement of meeting someone new after six years of being with her son's father. That relationship ended. She was left brokenhearted. She had made herself available to the guy, and he accepted what was being offered, with no strings attached. He never intended on leaving his girlfriend and two small children, which Maria knew of before entering into the relationship with him. In spite of that, she chose to stay in a relationship with him for the next two years. The relationship ended abruptly, when the guy and his family relocated to his hometown. She was twenty-five years old at the time of their breakup.

After their split up, Maria became sexually and mentally involved with yet another guy. But this time, it was slightly different than before. The twist came when they decided to move in together. Maria had never lived with a guy before. The truth is, she had never lived on her own. Maria and her son had been living with her mother since the child was born, and she was ready for a change.

By now, Maria had fallen into a pattern of being drawn to toxic relationships. She had a desire to be married, but the guys she was attracting were not marriage material.

Maria was the type of girl that would stay in unhealthy relationships until it either hurt too bad to continue or the guy dropped her. Hurting too bad to continue could mean a number of things, ranging from being physically, mentally, or verbally abused, them cheating, not committing, not loving her, and the list goes on and on.

Consequently, she stayed in that relationship for the next five years of her life.

When their relationship ended, Maria felt so alone. She was ashamed of herself, literally ashamed of herself. As a result, she became extremely shy. She had very low self-esteem. She had an inferiority complex. It was hard for her to hold her head up or look eye to eye with anyone.

Maria had been raised in a Christian home environment, and one of the things she remembered her mother frequently saying was "I do not want you to make the same mistakes I made." She was speaking of the premarital relationships that she herself had been involved in that resulted in a lot of heartache, pain, and distress. Being tied to the wrong person could take years from your life that you could never recover. Her mother had suffered the consequences of being tied to the wrong person.

So she knew having sex outside of marriage was wrong. She was taught about abstinence. She just did not know the reasons for abstinence. She did not know the consequences in the details of it or the price she would have to pay for not abstaining. But she did pay, boy, did she pay. She paid with having a child out of wedlock. She paid in suffering abuse from her former lovers. She paid with time—many years of her life wasted. She paid with money.

One of the things that each of Maria's past relationships had in common, other than all of them being toxic, was they all left her feeling smaller and emptier than the previous one.

At the age of thirty, Maria was at her wits' end. She was so sad and lonely inside. She decided to give her fragmented life to the Lord. She had made such a mess of things, and she knew that she would not be able to fix things on her own. All the heartaches and all the pain had driven her back to church. She became a Christian. It wasn't until then that she began to learn and understand what a soul tie was.

Soul Ties

What then are soul ties? you ask. A soul tie is an attachment. It ties one soul to another. Soul ties can be formed through marriage, through close friendships, and through sexual relationships. However, the most common soul tie is formed through sexual relationships. That type of soul tie is formed outside of marriage commitment. They have the tendency to bind together what you want, what you think, and what you feel to another. When two souls mingle, something from each person is imparted during the mingling. The two souls become one flesh through that mingling. Disconnecting from that person becomes difficult and requires great courage. It is like weaning a baby from his mother's breast or from his bottle. First, you take the bottle or discontinue giving the baby the breast. Then you introduce the sippy cup. The baby either accepts the sippy cup or rejects it. Not to worry, because when the baby gets hungry or thirsty enough, he will eventually take the cup. Next, the baby cries consistently day and night for about a week for his bottle or the breast. This process could take longer or even be shorter; it depends totally on the baby and the parents. Because sometimes, for peace's sake, the parent will give in to the baby's demand and give the baby what he wants. Thus, when the baby gets hungry or thirsty enough, he will eventually take the cup. Even though this still will not remove or replace the memory of the bottle or the breast, it will pacify the baby temporarily. The only thing that can permanently remove or reduce the memory of it is time. After an allotted amount of time has passed, the baby will adapt to the change and move on. But in some cases, you may still see a five-year-old sucking on his pacifier or even a bottle. This is why it is very important to know who you are bonding with before you commit sexual acts with them. What if the other person's soul is unhealthy? Simply saying, what if what they want, what they think, and what they feel is not normal?

Maria and Ken

Ten years had gone by, and Maria was still single. She was waiting on God, along with all the other single women at her church, waiting on God to supply the husbands. The only thing is that no one knew when God was going to show up with husbands in his hands. It is a fact that in most churches, the women exceed the men membership at least ten to one. So whenever a single male came to church, there were at least ten or more women to choose from in his age range. Sometimes this could be overbearing for a guy that's truly seeking the Lord. He may be forced to leave before actually getting what he went for. He came to church to escape the traps of women and to avoid running into more deceptions.

Just when it was looking like she was never going to meet anybody, she met Ken while attending a Fourth of July celebration at her girlfriend's house. They were introduced by a mutual friend. There seemed to be a strong chemistry between the two of them. A few weeks later, she received a phone call from the mutual friend, telling her that the guy had called asking about her. Maria consented to the request of her friend, giving him her phone number, and later that evening, she received a call from him. Maria did not know it at the time, but the next six years of her life would be like an emotional roller coaster for her. Up and down, break up to make up. She had entered into an emotional attachment with Ken, a soul tie. The kind of tie that is not easily broken.

Ken was very truthful with Maria about his expectations of their relationship. He put his cards on the table by telling her up front that he wanted a sexual dating relationship with her. While Maria did not verbally agree with Ken's demands, she did not object to them either. However, Maria never communicated to Ken what her expectations of their relationship were. She thought it was a given. Ken knew she was a Christian. He knew that she was celibate and had been celibate for the past ten years. She was correct in her thinking. Ken was fully aware that Maria was holding out for a husband. But since she did not communicate that to him, he acted as though he didn't know it. So after about five months of talking and getting to know one another, their relationship became a dating sexual relationship. Somewhere in Maria's mind, she thought that Ken would fall in love with her and eventually ask to marry her. But that never happened.

Although Maria was having sexual relations with Ken, she never renounced her relationship with the Lord. She continued going to church and serving in the ministry. What she was doing was wrong. The consequences of it left her with a lot of feelings of guilt and condemnation. But deep inside, God was still the most important thing in her life. Giving up on Him would never be an option.

Maria noticed that after they started having sexual intercourse, their relationship entered into a pattern. It seemed as though every three months, they would break up. It was three months together followed by three months apart. Sometimes she would break it off with Ken, other times he would break it off with her. Maria knew in her heart that Ken did not love her. Yet she would always take him back, allowing him to continue manipulating and controlling her.

Ken had never promised her a ring or an exclusive relationship with him, so he continued seeing other women throughout their relationship. There were times when Maria would put her feet down and withhold sex from Ken, thus giving him an ultimatum to either be in her life exclusively or out of her life permanently. But it never worked. Ken had made it known to her that he had many other options and someone else would gladly do what she wasn't willing to do.

Weaning Attachments

Finally, after six years of ups and downs, ins and outs, Maria decided to end the relationship with Ken forever. He had mistreated her so badly throughout the years. For her to continue in the madness any longer would be detrimental to her health and overall well-being. Yet she still felt as though she was being forced to let go. But she was willing to take the necessary steps to go through the process of letting go. Still, in doing that, she did it in hopes of Ken realizing that he truly loved her and how life for him would be unbearable without her. But that never happened. Ken's willingness to let her go without a fight broke her spirit even more. Ken never looked back. Maria couldn't look ahead. She still wanted Ken. She was still very much in love with him. She wanted so desperately for Ken to want her. From time to time, she would call him, crying over the telephone, hoping he would feel sorry for her and come back. But that never happened. Each and every time she made a decision to end the relationship with Ken, he agreed to it. For as long as Maria could remember, Ken had never made the first attempt to contact her after their split-ups. She would always get lonely and call him up. Thus, Ken would come back with nothing to offer other than a sexual dating relationship.

Maria realized that it would take God to sever the ties of her broken relationship and mend the fragments of her broken heart. It was not in her power to do so. But because she had failed God, she lacked the confidence in Him to see her through.

Ken had literally kicked her to the curb. In her own eyes, she looked inferior and insecure. There was a certain sadness and loneliness about her now. She felt opened and ashamed. Maria thought that anyone beholding her could see her humiliation. She felt diminished as a woman, diminished in her relationship with God.

It is a choice; who we love is a choice that belongs to you and me. Maria chose to love Ken. It was not as though Ken had been so good to Maria, because he had not. It was more because of the familiarity. She would always seem to attract the same type of men. They would have a different name and a different face, but they were the same man. Maria had spent so many years in deadbeat relationships, years that could never be restored.

Today, seven months after their breakup, Maria still longs for Ken. They talk periodically over the telephone, and Ken's offer still stands. However, Maria is determined more than ever to never look back. She has come to realize that God still loves her, God still wants her. Behind closed doors, she's moving on with a broken heart. She's taking it like a man and playing hurt.

ASIA'S STORY

This is the story of a young girl named Asia. Asia grew up in Savannah, Georgia. She and her siblings were raised by both of their parents. All their material and physical needs were met. They lived in a nice middle-class neighborhood. They drove the fanciest cars, ate at the best restaurants, and went on family vacations once a year.

One hot summer day in July, Asia's mother was sitting in the living room, looking out the window at a weeping willow tree, and reminiscing about a conversation she had with Asia.

"Asia, Asia," her mother called out to her daughter, who was in her bedroom, playing with paper dolls.

"In a minute, Mom," Asia yelled back. Within minutes, she was standing in front of her mother in the living room. "Yes, ma'am," she replied.

"What were you doing, honey?"

"I was playing with my paper dolls, pretending we were models and living in New York City in a penthouse."

From the time Asia was six years old up until she was around thirteen years old, she spent hours in her room on a daily basis, playing with her paper dolls. Playing with her paper dolls was her way of escaping and living out her dream. She would dress them and undress them, pretending they were her. She'd imagine herself with the fancy clothes and walking the runway, smiling and waving at her beholders.

Because Asia was easy on the eyes, her mom thought that she would be perfect as a model. So throughout her childhood, she was being fashioned for modeling or acting. Asia and her mom constantly talked about her someday becoming a model or maybe a Broadway star in New York City. This had been their dream for her since she was about ten years old. Asia grabbed hold of it, and in her imagination, she was a Broadway star.

Being the only girl in the family, Asia was spoiled rotten. There was not much she ever wanted that she did not get. To those on the outside looking in, it seemed as if her mother worked just to give her daughter everything she wanted. Her child-rearing skills were not the best. Her personal belief was to provide for your children the things that your parents could not provide for you. The most important thing to her mother was money and all the wonderful things it could buy. Therefore, one of her best attributes was spending money. She would always buy the best things her money could buy—cars, furniture, clothes, jewelry, and lots of toys. It was like Christmas every day in their household! Their house was the place to be. Her parents entertained at home a lot. This resulted in Asia having access to alcohol and cigarettes at an early age. So for the fun of it, she started smoking and drinking the gin and vodka her parents left hanging around the house. Even though her brothers did not participate in the drinking and smoking with Asia, they would not tell their parents either.

Asia and her two brothers attended the local public schools of Savannah, Georgia. She had just finished her last year at Bartow Elementary School during the fall of 1974 and would be attending Hubert Middle School next year. She was so excited!

Asia and her family were preparing for their trip to Jacksonville, Florida, for the summer to visit their relatives. Although she was thoroughly excited about going to Florida, she was even more elated about returning to Savannah that fall, going to middle school, and experiencing freedom from her snoopy brothers.

Summer had ended, and they were back in Savannah. Middle school was fun, changing classes, dressing out for PE and the drama club that Asia had enrolled in. The drama club was an after-school class Asia enrolled in that met twice a week, on Tuesdays and Thursdays. Both of her parents worked from nine to five and then some.

While Asia was at drama club on Tuesdays and Thursdays, her brothers would go to the Hudson Hill neighborhood center's afterschool program. Some evenings when the drama club class was cancelled, Asia and her friends would go to her house to drink alcohol and have sex. But before her parents came home, she would go to the community center and pick up her brothers. Because of her parents' busy lifestyle, they did not notice many of the changes that their daughter was going through. Asia managed to keep her grades up enough to get promoted to the next grade. She was never really an A student, so this was not an alarm to her parents.

Six years had passed, and it was the summer of 1980, and Asia had just gotten promoted to the twelfth grade. That summer, she went to Florida by herself. She stayed at her grandparents' house for a week but spent the rest of the summer with her aunt, uncle, and cousins. One hot Saturday night, Asia and her cousin attended a house party that her cousin's friend was throwing. That is when she met him, Eric. Eric was a twenty-nine-year-old drug trafficker from New York. He had come to Jacksonville two years earlier because he'd gotten into some trouble with the NYPD. It was Eric who would later introduce her to cocaine.

Almost immediately after meeting Eric, Asia fell for him, that New York accent and all. Eric was a good-looking man. Asia had never dated anyone as old as Eric before. That night, they talked, danced, drank together, and before the night was over, they exchanged phone numbers. A whole day had gone by, and Eric had not called Asia, so she took the initiative and called him. After a brief conversation, they met later that day at a nearby park. The rest of the summer was only Eric and Asia; her cousin hardly saw much of either one of them.

Asia had told Eric of her dreams of moving to New York City and perhaps becoming a Broadway star or doing some modeling. Savannah was smothering her, and she couldn't see anything good or big happening in Savannah. So Eric promised to one day take her to New York and introduce her to some of his friends that could help make her dreams a reality. Eric's talk pleased Asia.

Summer was almost over, so Asia and Eric made promises to stay in contact with each other. Asia promised Eric that she would come back to see him every other weekend. Eric's promise to her was "When you graduate from high school, I'll take you to New York City."

Eric and Asia kept in contact with each other as promised. She visited him in Florida as much as her parents allowed it. Of course, they did not know of Eric; they were merely letting her spend weekends with her cousin. Because she would be graduating and possibly going off to college in the fall, they did not mind giving her the space.

During one of her visits to Florida, Asia let her cousin in on their plans to move to New York City after she graduated from high school. Asia and Eric's planned date to leave for New York City was July 31, 1981. Her cousin agreed to keep the secret, and their plans progressed.

Asia kept her dream of moving to New York City and becoming a Broadway star or top model before her.

The 1980 through 1981 school year was quickly approaching, so Asia and her parents were meeting the final obligations for her graduation ceremony and planning a ceremony dinner for their family and friends.

Since Asia's grades were average, her parents thought it would be best if she attended a junior college for a year then later apply at a university. The plan was for her to move to Florida with her grandmother and attend Florida Community College of Jacksonville that fall and, after completion, transfer to a university.

It was spring, and graduation day had finally arrived! Oh, the joy that filled the atmosphere! Her parents were so proud of their daughter! They had never let the secret out about their plan to buy her a car as a graduation present. Her father had already purchased the car; it was a used Ford Escort. He was so proud! The car was in good condition, and it would bring her safely home on weekends from Florida. However, because Asia did not know about the car when they made their plans, the car ended up being left in Florida while they drove Eric's SUV to New York City.

The weekend of July 31, 1981, had arrived at last. Asia had already packed her things the night before. That morning, she kissed her parents and said good-bye as they were still lying in bed. They did not anticipate what was going to happen next. No, they did not have a clue that their daughter would be running off to New York with her twenty-nine-year-old boyfriend.

Once she arrived in Jacksonville, they loaded her things in Eric's SUV, said good-bye, and left for an almost seventeen-hour journey to New York City.

New York, New York, Big City and Dreams

Seeing New York City for the first time was dreams come true for Asia. She had never seen anything like it before in her life. The skyscrapers! The tall buildings! Her coming from a small town like Savannah, whose population was only 141, 654, did not prepare her for New York City. Everything was new and exciting! They walked faster, talked faster; they even thought faster.

Waiting for their arrival was Eric's sister Alaina, who lived in Melrose, a section of the Bronx in New York City. Asia and Eric had planned on moving in with her and her children until they got on their feet. While living there, Asia would apply for public assistance and low-income housing.

After about two weeks, Asia phoned her mother and told her that she had moved to New York City with her boyfriend Eric. Her mother cried and tried to encourage Asia to come home to her family. Asia explained to her mother that New York City was home for her now, and Eric was her family. Although Asia missed her mother very much, her place was with Eric now, seeing that she was pregnant with their first child. But she did keep in touch with her family.

Three years had passed, and Asia had not landed a role on a Broadway production yet. She had tried out for several stage plays, but because of a lack of experience, she didn't make the cut. Eric, on the other hand, could not find suitable employment for the lifestyle that he was used to living, because of his police record, so he got back into the drug ring. It wasn't long before they were using more of the drugs than he was selling. He had gotten in trouble with the big guys on so many occasions because of his drug use. Their lifestyle had quickly become a very dangerous one. They were getting robbed at gunpoint. Eric was getting busted by the NYPD and spending time in jail. Once during a drug bust, their children were taken from their home and had been placed in temporary shelter. Asia had to enroll in a drug rehab program for three months before the state would reevaluate her case and consider placing her children back in her custody. She had proven to the state that she was fit to get her children back by finishing the drug rehab program, obtaining employment, and staying clean. So she was awarded the custody of her children.

Walking the Streets of New York City

Needless to say, Asia's drug habit had gotten worst. Eric had misused so much of the big guys' money and drugs that he was almost beaten to death. No one would take a chance on him selling for them anymore. He was nothing but a drug addict. He had started robbing drug traffickers and stores to support their habit. He had even coerced Asia into prostituting to make money to support their habit. From time to time, she would take jobs, dancing in some of the strip clubs. One particular night in September, they were in their apartment using drugs, after Eric had held up a liquor store. The NYPD came in and arrested everyone that was in the apartment. Eric was given fifteen years to life in prison. Asia's kids were taken, and she lost her public housing. At this point, Asia was homeless. She called her mother, and her mother sent the money for a plane ticket home. But Asia used the money for drugs. Her excuse was that she did not want to leave her children in New York City. She would not leave without them. Once again, she enrolled into a drug rehab program and met the objectives to possibly regain the custody of her children, which wasn't enough this time, because she did not have income or adequate, safe housing for them. Losing custody of her children and not being able to see them left a damaging impact on her. As a result, she used the drugs more than ever now and did whatever it took for her to get them. The drugs numbed the pain and made the aching in her soul bearable.

So there she was, walking the streets of New York City. She was sleeping in old abandoned buildings. She frequently phoned home for money, and her mother would try talking her into coming home, but Asia wasn't ready yet. One night, a drug trafficker called her mother in Savannah because Asia owed him money and couldn't pay. He threatened to take her life if her mother did not send the money, so her mother wired the money to him that night. Following that incident, Asia agreed with her mother and Eric's sister on returning to Savannah, finding a job, and cleaning herself up, then returning to New York City and appealing her case with the state in order to regain the custody of her children.

Her mother was looking forward to Asia's arrival at Savannah/ Hilton Head International Airport. This was the first time that she saw her daughter since 1985. After their second child was born in October of '85, Asia flew home so that her mother could see her grandchildren. It was shocking to see that in just two short years, her daughter had seemed to deteriorate. Her mother wept inside.

Soon after Asia was settled into her parents' house, they assisted her in finding a job. Later, she enrolled in a local drug-and-rehab treatment program. Cleaning herself wasn't easy for Asia, but it was doable, as long as she kept her goal before her eyes.

Six months had passed, and Asia managed to stay clean. She was no longer using the crack cocaine. However, she was drinking beer and some other spirits. In July of 1988, Asia got sick with pneumonia and had to be admitted into the hospital. That was when she found out that she had full-blown AIDS. Asia did not let that stop her. She was still determined to win custody of her children back from the State of New York City.

After she remained clean for a year, she appealed her case with the Department of Children and Families in New York City but was denied custody. A disappointed Asia flew back to Savannah to continue in her treatment programs, and on a later date, she would return to make a third appeal to the courts for her children. But Asia never made it to that third appeal. She died in a local hospital at the age of twenty-nine.

After the funeral, Asia's mother was sitting in the living room, looking out the window at that big old weeping willow tree, remembering the conversation she had with her daughter on that hot summer day in July.

"Asia, Asia," her mother called out to her daughter, who was in her room playing with her paper dolls.

"In a minute, Mom," Asia yelled back.

SISSY'S STORY (BORN INTO A FAMILY)

We were all born into families. It was not our choice to pick the family that we were born into. Our parents came together, and as a result, we are here. What can we expect from the families that we are born into? Can we assume that our mother will always be there to nurture and care for us? Will we be expecting our father to provide for and protect us? Will we look forward to having an older brother that we can look up to or an older sister to be our best friend? What about an uncle to trust in like a father or maybe just a cool cousin that we would love to hang out with? What do we expect from our families?

Many of us grew up watching television families such as the *Brady Bunch*, *Good Times*, *My Three Sons*, and the list goes on. We would imagine being born into those types of families as we sat and watched. A lot of us observed our friends and their relationships with their family and wished we were born into that family. Some little black girls wished they were born into white families so that they could have the long blonde hair.

It is important for all of us to know that there is no perfect family. No, not one! The grass always looks greener on the other side. In most families, regardless of your race, the side of town you were raised on, or if you are rich or poor, secrets hide in families. Some of them are told eventually, but many are left untold.

This story is about a little girl named Sissy, who was violated at the age of eight. She wasn't violated by a stranger, because at an early age, she was taught the dangers of entertaining strangers. Sissy was violated by someone that she loved and presumed that they would protect, provide care, and love her.

Incest

Incest is sexual contact between persons who are so closely related that their marriage is illegal (e.g., parents and children, uncles or aunts and nieces or nephews). This usually takes the form of an older family member sexually abusing a child or an adolescent. The definition is taken from Rape, Abuse and Incest National Network (RAINN).

"Happy Birthday, Sissy! It's a girl!"

The hospital room was bursting with excitement! Her mom, dad, and older siblings were so proud that their newborn baby had finally arrived! There were others that joined in the celebration of new life with them, both sets of Sissy's grandparents, her aunts, uncles, and cousins. She went from arm to arm! "Be careful. Hold her head. Don't drop her," Sissy's mom proclaimed nervously. The spirit of life, love, and family connection filled the room. No one could have ever known or even imagined at the time that it would be one of them that would drop her.

Eight Years Later

Summertime is here, and Sissy, Bubba, and their parents are on their way to Grandma Alice's house. The kids usually spend two weeks of the summer with their grandparents. Normally, it's the week leading up to the Fourth of July. Their parents would drop them off and join them later for the picnic on the Fourth of July.

Sissy and Bubba looked forward to their summer with Grandma Alice. She would spoil them rotten. Her youngest son, Junior, would sometimes get jealous of the special treatment. Junior was spoiled himself, being the last of six older siblings. He was eighteen now and had just graduated from high school. His plans were to stay at home for at least a year and later join the USMC.

That summer was no different than the others. The gang and their offspring all gathered for the Fourth of July barbecue at Grandma Alice's house. They'd sing, dance, and eat much barbecue! The children would either take an outdoor shower or they would all cram into a small pool that someone had bought. That would be followed by the lighting of fireworks and everyone loading their vehicles and travelling home.

One particular summer, Sissy stayed at Grandma Alice's house alone. Bubba was old enough to play sports now, and it required him to be at football training camp during the month of July. She didn't mind going to Grandma's alone. It would be a lot of fun, plus she'd get all the gifts and a chance to earn all the money by helping with the chores.

Grandma Alice lived in a big old house located on a lot of land. It could sometimes get scary at night there. During the day, Sissy was fine. However, at night, she did become a little frightened. She just wasn't used to sleeping in the big spare bedroom alone. Sissy and Bubba usually shared that room. Besides that, Sissy remembered the scary stories that her mom, uncles, and aunties had told her of their experiences as children growing up there.

One night, after supper, Sissy and her uncle Junior were watching a scary movie together. After the movie had gone off, Sissy was frightened. It was then that her uncle Junior noticed her fear and decided to capitalize on it. He began by telling her the scary stories about their house and the stories associated with the bedroom she slept in. This made Sissy all the more frightened. She was so afraid. She did not want to sleep in that room alone that night or ever again. So she asked her grandma Alice if she could sleep in the room with her uncle Junior. Her grandma didn't see anything wrong with it. She knew that this was Sissy's first time sleeping in the room by herself. Therefore, she agreed.

That night, Sissy and her uncle Junior talked more about ghost stories. They were up well into the night. When her uncle Junior had finally gone to sleep, Sissy was still awake. She snuggled in close to him and finally drifted off to sleep herself. The next night was sort of the same as the night before. Sissy ended up sleeping with her uncle Junior. They played a lot that night. He pretended to be a monster, to keep her frightened and clinging to him. He teased and tickled her. He tickled her under her arms and in her belly. Then he started to tickle her roughly between her legs. That behavior continued on for about two nights.

Sissy was not alarmed by what was going on between her and Uncle Junior, because she had never been touched between her legs before. The only thing is that it left her kind of sore down there. The next night, they played the tickle game again, but this time, he put his hand inside her panties and tickled her. Sissy was beginning to feel uncomfortable with her uncle Junior. "Have you ever had a boyfriend kiss you or touch you between your legs?" Her reply was no. Then he started putting his tongue in her mouth and asking her if she liked what he was doing to her. Her reply was no, because it hurts. Surprised by her reply, he threatened to let her sleep in the ghost bedroom by herself if she told anyone about what he was doing to her.

The next day, Grandma Alice noticed that Sissy's behavior was sort of standoffish. "Are you okay, Sissy?" she asked. Sissy told her grandma that she was okay, but she really wasn't. She was frightened. Her genitals were sore, and she had a stomachache. Besides that, she didn't know what tonight would be like for her. Sissy had had enough; she was ready to go home.

A week had already passed, and in a few short days, her mom would be coming to take her home. One night, while she was in bed with her uncle Junior, he pulled out a magazine with pictures of nude men and women in it. While he was excited about the things they were doing to each other in the magazine; Sissy was confused. Later that night, she was introduced to oral sex.

That last week of summer vacation seemed like a month. But it was finally over. Her mom would be picking her up in the morning. Sissy knew in her heart that she never wanted to come to Grandma Alice's house again, especially without Bubba.

That summer changed her life forever. She didn't feel like a carefree little girl anymore. She was depressed and moody, which resulted in her being mostly withdrawn from everyone. However, her mom did notice a change in her daughter's behavior and became concerned. "Is everything all right with you, Sissy?" she asked. Sissy wanted to reveal everything that her uncle Junior had done to her that summer, but she was too frightened. She wanted to run into her mom's arms and be a little girl again. She so desperately needed to feel her mom's love and protection. But she remembered her uncle's threats of what would happen if she told anyone. He had told her that no one would believe it and that everyone would know what a nasty little girl she was. His words strutted through her mind. So Sissy kept silent. "I'm okay," she assured her mom.

One morning after returning home, Sissy went into the bathroom to discover that there was blood in her panties. She was devastated. Instead of telling her mom, once again she kept silent and hid the panties in a drawer in her room. That night, when Sissy was in the bathroom preparing for a bath, her mom walked in, and it alarmed Sissy. It was then that her mom saw the bloody panties. Now it made sense, Sissy's behavior since coming home. Her daughter was not a little girl anymore. She was becoming a woman.

The Birds and the Bees

After the incident with the bloody panties, Sissy's mom made a note to talk to her daughter about the changes that were taking place in her body. She talked to Sissy about her menstrual cycle and about the birds and the bees. Then very sternly, she concluded by saying, "Don't let anyone touch you down there." Her mom's last command made her more afraid than ever. It made her believe in the lies that Uncle Junior had told her, how everyone would think she's a nasty little girl. She wouldn't dare tell anyone now. How could she? She thought, *I have already broken that rule when I let Uncle Junior touch me down there.* So she kept silent and didn't go out that door.

WHAT? ARE YOU AFRAID OF—?

Fear is a feeling of alarm or disquiet caused by the expectation of danger, pain, disaster, terror, or dread. It is a state or condition. Fear is a vital response to physical or emotional danger. Fear is considered a strong survival instinct. If we couldn't feel fear, we couldn't protect ourselves from legitimate threats.

When we are confronted with new situations, circumstances, or people, we are likely to feel fear. We would much rather run back to what we are used to than face the unknown. People stay in miserable situations and relationships because of the fear of the unknown. They are petrified of change.

Everybody at some point in their lives experience feelings of fear. The truth is, we cannot control the feeling of fear. Furthermore, the feeling of fear will never go away.

Some of us are brave and have the courage to confront our fears, thus becoming very powerful people. While others are stuck and cannot move forward because they have allowed their fears to paralyze them, and their results is an unproductive life.

So I ask the question *what* with astonishment. Are you afraid of—?

Are you afraid of dying or growing old? Are you afraid of being alone? Are you afraid of what the future holds or are you afraid of change?

Behind this next door, I am going to tell chronicles of several individuals and their response to fear.

Fear of the Unknown

Everyone has fears. Fear is innate. Two of the most common fears to men are the fear of the unknown and the lack of power to control our final destinies. We are only human. We do not know how our story will end. We compare our selves to other people in our family or on our job that may have certain similarities to ours. As an example, if our parents died prematurely of a certain disease, usually around the same age of their death, we develop a fear of following in their footsteps. As a result, we start an intense diet-and-exercise program as a means of preventive care, when we are around their age at death. However, the truth remains the same, we do not know how our story will end, and the older we get, the greater that reality becomes.

Of course in some instances, we can prepare for the kind of future we desire to possess. Case in point, if our desire is to become a doctor, then we spend many years in med school, working to make it happen. If it is our aspiration to be a lawyer, we attend law school for numerous years, take the bar exam, and thus, we become lawyers. In such set of circumstances, we can pretty much tell how our story will end.

But how can you prepare for the unknown?

Most of the unknowns are the unwanted. However, they are not in our power to control. Therefore, right in the middle of life, life happens. Life happens with or without our permission or our consent.

What do you do when things are not turning out the way you wanted them to? What can you do to prevent an untimely death or accident? Can you stop the aging process? If we knew what tomorrow would bring, would we even desire to live past today?

Have you ever wondered, *what's going to happen to me when I'm older? Who will take care of me if illness suddenly overtakes me? Will my children place me in a nursing home? What will happen to me if I can't provide for my family anymore, while I'm yet a young man? What will happen to my children, if they are left motherless?*

Somewhere in the corridors of our mind, we hold images of a destined end that we are afraid may happen. Even though we are uncertain if it will come to pass or not, it could be the fear of dying a certain type of death. Maybe your mother had breast cancer and you hold that image in your mind and you are afraid that, like your mother, you will have breast cancer too. Perhaps all the men in your family had heart attacks around fifty-five, and you are fifty-four and a half. Most doctors support that theory. They believe that we are vulnerable to some of the illnesses and diseases that occur in our immediate family. Normally, before a doctor gives a diagnosis, he or she wants to know your family history.

Our current status might be rich, young, fine, or beautiful. But if we keep living, we will get old and become feeble and not so beautiful. Our family life may well be thriving today! Who could ask for anything more? We are married to the person we love and adore. Our children are all well and lovely. We got money in the bank. We're living on top of the world! Even so, that is not how our story ends.

Oh, what a difference a day makes. Our yesterday might have been fairly good and even unsurprising. We rose up early that morning and had breakfast with our loved ones. Then set out for work, school, or a doctor's appointment. Most of us travel the same routine. After work, we do the usual—travel home, perhaps get delayed in traffic, and then finally arrive at our final destination, which is home. Shortly thereafter, we eat dinner with our loved ones, do some cuddling, and prepare for the same predictable schedule tomorrow.

Our morning might have been the norm, and our evening could have turned out to be the norm, but what about the in-between, the midday? Inside our homes, behind closed doors, is where we deal with the real issues from unknown, unpredictable, and unscheduled events or announcements that we received perhaps in the middle of our day.

So let's unwind to see the difference a day makes.

Mary

Mary is a thirty-nine-year-old divorced mom. She is raising three children alone. Following the divorce with the children's father, she devoted her life and time to them. Her weekends and summers were usually the same— family outings, weekend getaways, or camping with her children. Yes, it would have been great to have their father participate in his children's life, but I guess that was asking too much. However, Mary picked up the slack and made up for the discrepancy. She made certain that the children did not miss a beat. Thus, Mary's relationship with her children and their home life was very important to her.

It was January 3, 2012, and Mary was on the way to her doctor's appointment. She had dropped the children off to school and still had time to stop by McDonald's to grab a cup of coffee. She really hated this time of the year—the time to get her annual, with the doctor poking, pushing, and inserting instruments in her. However, she was grateful, grateful that she had health insurance through her employers. Because, following the divorce, she was removed from her ex's insurance.

During the examination, the doctors discovered a lump in Mary's left breast. They scheduled a follow-up appointment for her to have a mammogram done. The earliest appointment was scheduled for two weeks away. So for the next two weeks, she lived in absolute turmoil. Mary was so worried. Her mother had lost a battle with breast cancer, and she had no idea of how this would turn out for her. A fear of the unknown gripped her heart.

So at this point, we see that her morning started off ordinarily. But who would have thought that by midday her life would be turned upside down?

Mary did not tell the children, or anyone for that matter, of the news from the doctor's appointment. She feared that if she told someone, they would look on her with pity and concern, which would result in her being even more afraid.

Although Mary was not a Christian, she did believe that there was a higher power. Thus, she began praying to a god that she did not know.

What about the Children?

All sorts of questions ran through her mind. *What will happen to my children if I'm not here to provide for them?* She wondered. *Who will help me through this, seeing that I am unmarried?* She felt so alone in the world. Her eyes were swollen with weeping.

Subsequently, every day for the next two weeks, she'd come home from work, cook, prepare the dinner for her children, then go in her room, and behind closed doors, she would weep.

Fear of Not Measuring Up

Have you ever felt like you didn't measure up or like you were just not fitting the bill? It could have been because of your own insecurities, or it may possibly be the result of someone you trusted that said you didn't measure up or treated you thus.

Sometimes the nonexistence of material things or the lack of money to provide the essential needs for your family can very well leave us feeling like we don't measure up.

Maybe you were not born as perfect as your siblings, or so you were told. You could have been called the black sheep of the family or the ugly duckling. Perhaps you were a fat kid or had buckteeth.

Quite often, we develop insecurities in our home, with our families. Be assured that you were not born shy, timid, or fearful. Those behaviors are taught early in our lives through our interactions with others.

In society today, our cultural differences, along with our race and gender, can result in us feeling like we don't measure up.

Two of the most common issues that are associated with the fear of not measuring up are you constantly comparing yourself to others and you settling for less than you deserve.

Shelley

The first person I would like to introduce to you is Shelley. Shelley has a fear of not measuring up. She suffered with low self-esteem throughout her childhood and most of her adult life. At a very young age, Shelley had no one to validate her, so as a result, she lived beneath her privilege. Most of us are attacked verbally in our homes by other siblings or by our parents. We also encounter verbal abuse from teachers and friends. These are the people we trust for validation. From a child's position, gaining the approval of family, friends, and teachers is extremely important. Thus, like any other child, she sought approval from her family, friends, and teachers. But she could never find a balance. When she won the approval of her family, she lacked the approval of some teacher. If she gained the approval of her teacher, she would lack the approval of her friends. When she did well in school, she lost friendships. If she misbehaved in school, she would lose the teacher's good favor. This brought about an inward turmoil for her. She was too concerned about what others thought about her.

Shelley was afraid that she would never measure up or gain validation from people. Her fears were seen in a lack of participation and enthusiasm. She had never taken on challenges or competed in anything. Shelley engaged in games or competitions just for the fun of it. If anyone attempted to make it more than just fun, she would quit.

Her fear of not measuring up could also be seen in her work ethics. She was a procrastinator. She would never meet deadlines.

Shelley had never fully given herself to anything. Not to school, not to relationships, not on the job, and not to her dreams. She was afraid that if she did, it wouldn't be good enough or someone else would beat her out. Someone else looked better, talked better, or would do a better job. She was stuck on average or below average. If ever she'd put forth an effort to do her best, look her best, or be her best, people would take notice. But immediately after a high performance, fear would set in, and she'd become afraid of a time that had not even come yet. She would be afraid that people would expect more from her, and what if she couldn't measure up to her last performance? So she would do just enough to get by the next time.

Consequently, Shelley lived within the stronghold of low self-esteem and insecurity. She continuously measured herself by herself and by the standards of others. Behind closed doors, she was sad, lonely, insecure, and downright scared. Her fear of not measuring up affected every area of her life. It had an effect on relationships with the opposite sex, her job, and her family life.

She sank deep in a hole of despair, constantly feeling as if her relationships were in jeopardy by other women. She didn't feel pretty enough, tall enough, or that her hair was long enough to hold her man's attention. Sorry to say, most guys don't stick around long enough to pull you out of the hole of despair.

The reality is, there will always be someone younger, prettier, or someone that dresses better or someone that does it better. But what are you going to do about you, your gifts, abilities, and qualities?

In the workforce, Shelley would meet the minimum requirements. She would never exceed their expectations. If asked to do a difficult task, she would just make excuses to not do it or not show up.

Moreover, the fear of not measuring up showed in her family life. Since she had grown up being timid and fearful, Shelley was determined that her children would be all that they could be, or shall I say, all that she could not be because of her fears. She was trying to live her life through her children. But there is a danger in trying to live your life through your children. Shelley wasn't aware of what she was doing at the same time as it was happening. It wasn't until after they were grown up and moved out that she realized what she had done. Without knowing it, she had set very high standards for her children. As a consequence, the spirit of not measuring up rested heavily on their shoulders. It was as though anything they did to make an attempt to please her would never be enough. It was unfeasible to satisfy her. Even when they gave their absolute best, it was not good enough. Her disapproval was heard in her voice tones, seen in her eyes, and felt by her withholding affection from them until their performance arrived at perfection.

Settling (Afraid of Not Getting What You Want)

Mamie

It was around nine thirty, Tuesday morning, and Mamie had only been to work an hour when she received the phone call from her friend. "You had better get here as soon as possible!" her friend exclaimed. "Mr. Landlord and the police are at your apartment, removing your things." Mamie was being evicted. However, she knew it was only a matter of time before it happened.

On May 1, 1999, she had received an eviction notice attached to the front door of the apartment where she was living. Mamie hadn't paid her rent, as agreed upon, in three months to date. She just couldn't afford it anymore. After paying her car note, car insurance, utilities, and gas fare, she didn't have much left from the income she earned from her job. She was just staying there, buying time until she could figure out what to do.

Besides that, Mamie was familiar with the four basic steps of the eviction process for the state of Florida. Step one, the tenant will receive a three-day notice to pay rent or vacate the property. If the rent money is not paid within the three days or the property is not vacated, the landlord proceeds to step two. In step two, the landlord files the documents under the county civil courts division. This process can take anywhere from three to ten business days. In step three, an eviction summons is served by the sheriff department. At that time, the tenant has five days to respond, stating their intentions to pay or vacate. One of three things will happen after this process: The tenant replies within the allotted five days and pays all the money needed to be current. The tenant replies to the judge but without the money. The tenant does not reply at all. Mamie chose option three. She did not reply at all. She did not have the money nor would she have it in thirty days.

Mamie made it home as quickly as possible. Most of her things were already sitting on the curb. At this point, she was homeless.

So there she was, sitting on the curb, with humiliation written all over her face. As she sat there, fanning flies, she began to look back over her life. *How did I get here?* she thought to herself. Mamie began reflecting on her childhood.

She was a beautiful, well-loved, and well-cared-for child. Her parents loved her very much, and she was accepted. Throughout her childhood, she was constantly told of how beautiful she was by her family, friends, and even strangers. Her smile would soften the heart of anyone beholding it. Mamie did not try to be beautiful; she was beautiful. It wasn't until later on in her life that Mamie would find out that being beautiful would cost her some things. It would cost her some friendships. She would become the envy of a lot of people's eyes. Her outer beauty caused people to either cater to her or be a hater of her.

During her primary years, she was a very happy little girl. She had lots of friends. Everyone seemed to enjoy being around her because of her pleasant disposition and innocence. Like most little girls, she wanted to be a princess when she grew up. Her prince would rescue her out of the clutches of evil villains trying to steal her joy. He would protect her from dangers to come. Most importantly, he would provide her with all the love, kisses, and praises she needed.

Mamie remembered being in high school. She remembered being on the cheerleading squad. She even remembered being despised by the other girls. It didn't matter what she did to try and fit in; they hated her even more. This was her first time ever feeling and experiencing such disconnect. High school is a very crucial time for a teenager, and being accepted by your peers is extremely important. Mamie did not know how to handle the rejection. All her adolescent friendships had died off. The majority of the girls that she used to hang out with were jealous of her now. She was always losing friendships over some boy.

It did not take long for Mamie to start putting the pieces together. Boys and men catered to her; girls and women shunned her.

As a young adult, Mamie was becoming accustomed to what was going on. Then she began to use what she had. Since the men flocked to her and made her feel loved, accepted, and favored, she flung to the men. Any man that would give her the love and attention she had when she was growing up was allowed in her inner circle. As a result, she would conform to their expectations. For many years, Mamie went from one relationship to the next. Man after man. They all used her. But among the women, she was an outcast.

Mamie wanted the same thing that every other woman wanted; she wanted a husband. She wanted to be loved and cherished. She wanted a knight in shining armor. But because of her past failures and the lascivious lifestyle she'd lived, she didn't feel like she was worthy of a good man. So she kept settling for less than she deserved. She spent numerous years engaged in one bad relationship after the other, until she met Pops. Pops was a seventy-two-year-old married man. He had children her age and older.

Their relationship became the most meaningful one she had ever experienced. Let me explain. Pops did many nice things for her. He purchased her a car. He spent time with her kids. He helped support them financially, meeting their basic needs and beyond. It was Pops who had helped her get into the apartment that they'd lived in for the past three years. Pops became a father, lover, provider, and husband to her. In many ways, he was her knight in shining armor, her rescuer. He had never discussed leaving his wife, and Mamie was okay with that. Her expectations from him were security, support, and provision. Thus, she provided for him sex and fun with a beautiful young woman.

Mamie could have never imagined what would happen next. She was totally taken by surprise at the news of Pop's death. Her heart was filled with anxieties. She wanted to blame somebody for the predicament that she was in. But she knew blaming someone else wouldn't help. She was in this bad situation because of a lot of wrongful choices she had made.

While sitting there on the curb, fanning flies, she was forced to see how poorly she had managed her life. *How can I tell my children we have no place to live? Is there an easy way to say we are homeless?* she questioned herself. With tears streaming down her face, Mamie just sat there, fanning flies.

SYLVIA'S STORY

Sylvia and Sydney had been involved for the past three years. They were introduced by a mutual friend at their job's annual Christmas party. They had both been working for the same company in different departments for the last ten years. Sylvia had heard a lot about Sydney, how he was a womanizer and all. She had known of him for at least fifteen years, and no woman seemed to have managed to hog-tie him down yet. Despite his personal life, most people had a lot of good things to say about Sydney. He's a homeowner. He's been employed at the plant for twenty-five years. He has an athletic build, and he's youthful looking. He's a very hard worker. Sydney was a jack-of-all-trades. Any woman would think that Sydney was a good catch. Nevertheless, one couldn't help but question that if he's that good, then why isn't he married? Good question, huh?

Although everything previously mentioned about Sydney's character was true, it was also true that he was a womanizer. He had his pick of any woman. Even as a young man throughout high school, Sydney was a womanizer. Sydney loved women. He studied women. While the average teenage boy spent their time on the basketball court or the football field, Sydney spent his summers fishing with older men. He would spend hours listening and learning master skills on how to get a woman, any woman. Older women taught him how to make senseless love to a woman. If he didn't know anything else, he knew how to turn a woman on and out. When he made love, he made love with a purpose.

He never had to go after women. Because of his kind nature and good looks, they would always flock to him. He never had to take any one woman seriously. If one of them called it quits or gave up on winning his heart, there was always someone who would gladly take him up. He could basically talk a woman into or out of anything.

When Sylvia met Sydney, he was in his forties, just around the age of a midlife crisis. So instead of slowing down, he was getting it started all over again. Their friendship escalated quickly. He learned her likes and dislikes. He listened to her voice tones to determine most of her likes and dislikes. As she spoke, he looked into her eyes and closely followed her facial expressions. Sydney learned the words that would make her laugh or make her cry. It didn't take long for Sydney to sweep Sylvia off her feet.

Sylvia had spent most of her life protecting herself by hiding her feelings. When she was hurting, she did not let it show. If she was angry, she would suppress the feelings. When she loved someone, she would not communicate it to them verbally. Sylvia became skilled at hiding her feelings. She was afraid of being hurt. But each and every attempt she made to protect herself failed, and Sylvia would end up getting hurt time after time. Therefore, by the time she met Sydney, she was through with protecting herself. Her plans were to break free from the past and love Sydney with everything that was in her. Hence, that was exactly what she did. No holds barred. For the first time in her life, she wasn't afraid to love. She held nothing back. She felt so elated and free! In her state of high excitement, she gave Sydney the best of her love! Sylvia let her guard down and loved Sydney with everything she had—her money, her time, and her body. Sydney selfishly received everything she had to offer, never giving anything in return, because the only thing Sydney wanted from Sylvia was her body. He was not after her heart or her love.

Their relationship lasted for about three years. Within that three-year period, Sydney never bought her flowers or did many public things with her. Most of their time spent together was at her house, at night, after ten o'clock. Behind closed doors, Sydney would make mad, passionate love to her! He made her body come alive for the first time in her life! Sylvia's eyes and nose were wide open! Occasionally, he would tell her he loved her. As a result, Sylvia threw all caution to the wind and, with everything she had, loved him back.

Within the last year of their relationship, the unexpected happened. Sylvia did not get her period for a month. She assured Sydney that it was probably nothing because she was having menstrual cramps. But after two months passed and she still didn't have a cycle, she decided to take a home pregnancy test. The test confirmed that she was indeed pregnant. Although she did not deliberately try and get pregnant from Sydney, it was good news to her. Later that night, she invited Sydney over and revealed to him the results of the pregnancy test. Sydney was quiet after receiving the news. So Sylvia began to cry. She wanted his child just as much as she wanted him. They had talked about having a baby before, and now surprisingly, she was pregnant.

When Sydney finally broke the silence between them, he began explaining to her that their unborn baby was just a blood clot, not a formed child. He continued by saying he did not want any more children at that time. Even though he had never proposed to her, he said that they would eventually get married and have a child out of that union. "But right now," he continued, "an abortion is the best option." Sylvia cried vehemently. She did not believe in abortions; she believed in the Bible and God. However, when it came to her personal convictions, her unborn baby, and the man she loved, Sylvia chose Sydney.

Sylvia contacted the abortion clinic to make the appointment to have the procedure done. Afterward, she filled Sydney in on the details, the date, time, and cost. Sydney never even offered to pay for the abortion. However, he did take her to the clinic.

It seemed like they would never arrive at the abortion clinic on that cold winter morning in December. A dreadful silence filled the car. Sylvia waited for Sydney's words, but he kept silent. She turned her head and looked through the passenger window to avoid eye contact with him. But she did not have power over the tears that were falling from her eyes. With her whole heart, she had loved Sydney, and she hoped he would see that in the sacrifice she was making for him. Sylvia was killing her unborn child for Sydney. She glanced at him out of the corner of her eye as he was wiping his eyes. They did not speak a word to each other, they just wept. They had both agreed to spend Christmas with their families and have the abortion after Christmas.

Later at the clinic, after Sylvia had checked in, the nurse called her to the back. As she followed the nurse, she looked back, and her hand threw a kiss from her mouth to Sydney.

In less than two hours, the procedure was over. Sylvia, still concerned about Sydney, sent a message to him through the nurse, letting him know that she was all right. She didn't want him to be sad or worried about her. Sylvia loved Sydney.

To cut a long story short, Sylvia and Sydney did not get married. They never had another child. Three months after the abortion, Sydney was dating the new lady at the office that worked in the same department as Sylvia. Even in that, Sylvia tried to hold on to Sydney with everything she had. But Sydney already knew everything Sylvia had, because she had already given it to him—her money, time, love, sex, and an unborn baby.

Sylvia's pain took no rest.

Later that same year, Sydney married the new lady at the office. Sylvia continued working there for about three years, and then she turned in a letter of resignation. Interesting enough, about two months after his marriage, Sydney started pursuing her again. He would call her at the house. He even offered her a sexual relationship with him. But Sylvia turned him down. Her heart bled for his new wife, who probably loved him as much as she had. It wasn't until that moment that Sylvia realized the kind of man Sydney really was. But realizing the kind of man he was did not cause her pain to go away or lessen it. It could not make up for her losses. She would never recover the time, the money, her self-esteem, the unborn child she gave up, or the years she spent loving him.

Rumor has it that the reason Sydney married so hastily was because his new wife had gotten pregnant. So I will pose the question, did he feel regret for dishonoring Sylvia during her pregnancy and influencing her to abort their unborn baby? Might this now be the reason he honored his new wife? Who can say?

MONEY CAN'T BUY ME LOVE

What defines a man or a woman? What are some of the attributes that one would use to describe a man or a woman?

The *American Heritage Dictionary of the English Language* defines a man as "an adult male human being, as distinguished from a female." It further defines a man as "a male human being endowed with such qualities as courage, strength, and fortitude, considered characteristics of manhood. He is a husband, a lover, a sweetheart."

Some attributes used to describe a man are his money, his being strong but gentle, thoughtful, and confident; and his being a provider and protector.

But what if he does not match all the above criteria? What if he has courage and strength but lacks gentleness? Is he still a man? What if he is doubtful or fearful but has a great deal of money? Is he yet a man? Is he still a man if he's never been married or fathered a child?

Do you remember the old saying "Having a piece of a man is better than having no man at all"? What is a piece of a man? When a man does not fall into a category or fit the description of what we think a man should be or what we think a man should have, what is he? Is he less than a man? Is he a piece of a man? Is having a piece of a man better than having no man at all? Do you take and break a man and divide up his body parts, his arm, his leg, his heart? Afterward, do you distribute the parts? My question is, what makes him a piece of a man and who decides which pieces you get? I suppose the individual determines which piece of the man is important to them and makes their decision based on that.

Do you keep a man when you know that he has been unfaithful to you? If the relationship is degrading and you're ashamed, do you keep him? Is having that man better than having no man at all?

Does having his name, his money, and his child make up for not having his heart or his love? Is having a piece of a man better than having no man at all?

What defines a woman, and what are some attributes used to describe her?

A woman is an adult female human being. She has a feminine quality or aspect. She is a wife, a mother, a homemaker. It is in her nature to love.

Attributes used to describe a woman are feminine, weak, soft, having a loving nature, and being a nurturer.

What if she is unmarried? Will she still be considered a woman? Women have always been looked at negatively in our society if they were not married and/or had children by a certain age. Some women choose not to have children. Also, some women choose to remain unmarried if they have been in a bad marriage before. If she does not have any children, is she not a woman? Still, there are other women who remain unmarried for religious purposes. So I ask you, without a husband and without a child, is she still a woman?

His-Story

Booker is a forty-year-old married man. All his life, he had worked hard to gain approval and acceptance from his family and peers. Booker sought endorsement from society, mentors, and protégés time after time. He was too overly concerned about others' opinion of him.

Booker was eighteen months old when his mom and dad split up. After their separation, he only saw his dad once, and Booker was three years old at that time. When he was five years old, his mother married his stepfather, and from their union came two siblings—a sister and a brother. His stepfather came from a family of strong men, strengthened by money, power, and prestige. So the bar was held high when it came to being a Coleman.

There were times in Booker's childhood that he felt like he didn't fit in. He didn't think of himself as being smart enough. In order for him to accomplish the things that he had, he pushed his self far beyond the limits of normal expectations. Nothing was given to him on a silver platter. He worked hard for his money. He worked even harder to keep it.

Throughout his childhood, Booker would often hear his stepfather say things like this: "A man gets out there and makes a living for his family," "A real man will do whatever it takes," "People will respect you, love you, and accept you when you have money," and "Money can get you everything you want, women, acceptance, and power."

So Booker got out there and made his mark in the world. He gained respect. He had power. He had his share of women. In spite of all that, he was still a very lonely man, because there was one thing, however, that his stepfather erred in not telling him, and that was money can't buy you love. After he had accomplished all the things that make a man a man, what will be his recompense?

At the end of the day, there was no one to share it with, because he had no one who really loved him.

There was a young woman from his childhood, his childhood sweetheart, Anna, whom he loved to a great extent. But since she did not meet the criteria of what he thought would be good for his self-image, he let her slip right out of his hands. Anna was a godly, virtuous woman. However, Booker thought he needed a trophy wife for his big ego and lifestyle. Anna was only an elementary-school teacher. But Booker was a man of power, prestige, and money. What Booker needed for his ego was a woman with power, prestige, and money, even though, it was Anna's shoulder he would run to cry on when he was at his wits' end. She would comfort and console him, literally love him back to health, and send him on his way.

At the age of thirty, he met and married Stephanie. Stephanie was a very beautiful and wealthy woman, who had come from a family of doctors and lawyers. She was indeed a trophy wife! There was no one in the world that Stephanie loved more than herself. She loved Booker but not with the kind of love a woman loves her husband with. She was so vain. Stephanie was so vain to the point that she didn't want to ruin her figure by having children. It was her friends who had convinced her that having a child was a guaranteed future investment. So for that reason alone, she gave him a child during their fifth year of marriage. She had also married for power, prestige, and money.

After their son was born, the unexpected happened. Suddenly, they felt an obligation to do the right thing. The couple decided to make a real go of their marriage for the child's sake. They both made positive advances for the well-being of their son.

When Stephanie first laid eyes on their son, she fell in love with him. She forgot all about the selfish reasons she had for not wanting to have a child in the first place.

He became her motivation for living. Money, power, and prestige had lost its hold on her. She was a mother now, and her son was the most important thing in her life.

Booker set out to find his natural father. He was only eighteen months old when his mom and dad went their separate way and had only seen him once since then, at the age of three. His mom never tried looking him up. After all, Mr. Coleman had legally adopted Booker and had given him his name. But Booker wanted his son to have his birthright name. He wasn't trying to hurt his stepfather or mom; he just wanted to have his legal name. Besides that, no one asked him how he felt about having his name changed. His mom thought that she was doing what was best for her son by not speaking much about his dad and raising him in a prosperous environment with well-qualified mentors. But if Booker would have been given a choice, he would have chosen to get to know his natural father. But he was not given a choice in the matter. His father's name was seldom spoken of in their household. When he did hear things about his dad, it was through his aunts, and it was never something positive. Booker made a vow to himself to always be there for his son. He vowed to have an active role in his life for as long as he lived.

Her-Story

Mary is a thirty-six-year-old self-made millionaire. She is an only child that was raised by her mom and grandma. Mary's father was not involved in her childhood, and to this day, she seldom sees him. At the tender age of eight, Mary started her menstrual cycle. It was devastating for her because she was so young. As Mary got older, she began suffering severe menstrual cramps accompanied by heavy bleeding. The older she got, the more severe the bleeding and cramps were. Her mom eventually scheduled a doctor's appointment to find out what was going on with her daughter. During the doctor's exam, Mary had an ultrasound that revealed that there were fibroid tumors on her uterus. Her doctor explained that he would need to schedule an appointment for a biopsy to determine whether the fibroid tumors were cancerous. She was very nervous when she went to her appointment to have the biopsy. After the biopsy was complete, Mary waited for a period of two days before calling the doctor's office to find out if it was benign. Her results came in benign. However, she would need to have the fibroids removed. Hearing that news was disturbing for Mary, she was only eighteen years old at the time. Mary, her mom, and the doctor discussed the type of surgery that she would need. Because the size of the fibroids was large, they would have to perform a complete hysterectomy. Mary and her mom agreed with the doctor's diagnosis and solution to the problem. But at that time, Mary did not understand fully everything that having the surgery would entail. She knew that she would never be able to have children, but at the age of eighteen, Mary wasn't thinking about having children anyway. She had her whole life ahead of her. Besides that, she was pretty glad to be done with her menstrual cycle and those awful cramps.

Immediately following the surgery, Mary experienced surgical menopause. She began feeling as though she was going through a hurricane. Once Mary survived the seemingly hurricane experience, she had to come face-to-face with the fact that she would never have children. For the next five years, she put all her energy into her college studies. The determination of her heart was to become a wealthy businesswoman. She supposed that becoming successful would alleviate the pain that came from not being able to have children.

After college, Mary went to work for a cosmetic company as an assistant manager. Even though she gave herself wholeheartedly to her job, it still did not fill the emptiness that came from being barren. So Mary started living a footloose, fancy-free lifestyle. Not being able to have children caused her to settle. She got involved in all sorts of relationships with men. She dated men with ready-made families. The most serious relationship she had only lasted for about a year and a half.

Being unable to conceive left Mary feeling incomplete as a woman, because having children was what made a woman a woman.

Mary continued rehearsing those old memories, when suddenly, she remembered that she hadn't texted her husband Allen to see if he had eaten dinner or if he wanted her to grab something before coming home. She had a craving for some seafood herself. It was late Friday evening and the end of another workweek. Allen did not respond to her text, which was kind of normal for the past six months. He would later reply, "I was busy," "I did not hear the phone, it was too noisy," or "I left the phone in the car." She knew his top three excuses by heart. They were committed to memory.

Mary knew that she would be stuck in traffic for at least thirty minutes, so she decided to call her mom. "Hello," she heard her mom's voice on the phone.

Hi, Mom.

"Hi, honey," her mom responded. Before Mary could get a word in, her mom continued. "How was your day, dear? What are your plans for the weekend?"

"I haven't made any plans. I'm waiting to hear from Allen."

"I don't know what to say about that husband of yours."

"Mom, I'm at my exit now. I'll call you once I get home." Mary rushed off the phone. She did not want her mom to start in on her about Allen.

Allen still had not responded to her text, so she decided to go on home and just eat a sandwich or something.

Pulling into their driveway, she noticed that Allen had not made it home yet. Mary peeled herself out of the car with all the work she hadn't finished at the office with her. Bringing the office home with her was normal for her. Working at home would keep her occupied until her husband came home. But lately, he had been getting home later and later.

Allen was one of eight children. He was the only male in his family that went off to college immediately following high school. Allen went to college on a four-year football scholarship. His parents loved each and every one of their eight children, but Allen was thought to be a special child, destined for greatness. At the end of his fourth year at college, Allen was injured. He had torn the ligaments in his right knee. He continued playing to finish up the season although he played hurt. Needless to say, the knee injury prevented him from making it to the big times—the NFL.

Allen did not go home right away after college because he felt as though he had let his family down. He couldn't bear to see the disappointment in their eyes. Even worse, he did not want them to see the hurt in his. Two years had passed, and Allen was barely getting by on the income he earned working at The Athletic Shop. So he called home to talk with his dad about the current situation he was in. Allen's dad told him how proud he was of him and said to him, "Son, come home." It was at that moment when Allen decided to return to his hometown and make a living, working for his dad's construction company.

Mary met Allen at an entrepreneur engagement that she was on program to speak at. She had been nominated as one of the who's who in entrepreneurship. She had made her way to the top of a cosmetic chain that resulted in her being a wealthy woman.

Allen, on the other hand, owned a small construction company that was very successful at the time. He had a healthy, wealthy viewpoint on life and his future. Allen had the answer to every one of the questions. To cut a long story short, Mary loved a man who knew what he wanted and knew what it would take to get it. Allen was that kind of man. Mary was intrigued! This man did it for her! He was a smooth operator. Yes, indeed a smooth operator! He walked the walk and talked the talk. Not to mention, he was easy on the eyes too. Their relationship progressed, and after about six months of dating, they got married.

Ten years had passed, and the excitement had worn off. The talk that used to turn her on now turned her off. They were just mere words. Allen talked the talk but could not walk the walk. His business never grew or became successful. He was always out chasing after another pipe dream. Allen was determined to make it to the top or die trying. Even though Allen married a wealthy woman, it still wasn't enough for him. There was an emptiness in him that no human could fill.

Maybe that is what Mary and Allen shared in common— they both had an emptiness that no one could ever satisfy.

It's hard to die to a dream, whether it is playing in the NFL or giving birth to a child.

Today, Mary spends most of her evenings alone. The truth of the matter is that Mary is still very much in love with Allen. But she had to come to terms with the reality that she would never be able to satisfy the longings of his soul. No matter how much money she had or how much she loved him, she could never truly conquer his heart. Money can buy a house, but it can't make the house a home. Money will attract many acquaintances, but it would not make them true friends. Money can't buy me love.

I STAND AT THE DOOR AND KNOCK

Have you come across your individual situation anywhere in this book, whether the abuser or the victim of abuse? Did you put your trust in someone, a parent or spouse, a significant other and they let you down? Maybe you haven't experienced any of it personally. Perhaps your friend or your sister suffered the abuse, and because you are knowledgeable about their pain, you're hurting as well. We have all gone through things, and some are yet going through things. The question is, will you continue to go through them by yourself, will you go through them with someone you don't trust, or will you go through them with Jesus? Jesus can meet the needs of your heart. You can trust Him. He is the permanent answer for your temporary problem. Jesus—He is the answer.

> I know your [record of] works and what you are doing; you are neither cold nor hot. Would that you were cold or hot! So, because you are lukewarm and neither cold nor hot, I will spew you out of My mouth! For you say, I am rich; I have prospered and grown wealthy, and I am in need of nothing; and you do not realize and understand that you are wretched, pitiable, poor, blind, and naked. Therefore I counsel you to purchase

from Me gold refined and tested by fire, that you may be [truly] wealthy, and white clothes to clothe you and to keep the shame of your nudity from being seen, and salve to put on your eyes, that you may see. Those whom I [dearly and tenderly] love, I tell their faults and convict and convince and reprove and chasten [I discipline and instruct them]. So be enthusiastic and in earnest and burning zeal and repent [changing your mind and attitude]. Behold, I stand at the door and knock; if anyone hears and listens to and heeds My voice and opens the door, I will come in to him and will eat with him, and he [will eat] with Me. (Revelation 3:15-20)

Even though the above letter is written to Christians, Christ is knocking at the door of all people's hearts. His grace is extended to anyone that will hear his voice and open the door. Listen, Christ is speaking.

I know your record, your past performances, and your highest achievements. I take note of what you are doing now. I know your works. I know that you are trapped in the truth about yourself, trapped in what happened to you. I know your educational status, your strategies, and self-efforts to maintain self-sufficiency. I know your works. You are trying to protect yourself, concealing evidence, trying to change yourself, and you are frustrated as a result.

Although you say everything is great, you are stagnated. Even you cannot see your barrenness. You are uncovered and unprotected. Therefore, let me encourage you to place your trust in me. Then you may be genuinely prosperous and have all grace abounding. All sufficiency, in all areas, at all times. Imagine that, nothing missing, nothing lacking, and nothing broken. Full coverage! I will clothe you!

What have you got to lose? You've tried it over and over again your way. You have trusted in people on behalf of your care and protection. You've even trusted in your money. Try me! Trust me with you.

I'm on the other side of the door, knocking. Open the door. Your life will begin to improve the moment you open that door. Everything you need is on the other side of the door. I'll give you rest from all your self-efforts, rest from all your works. Peace is at the door.

I'll be in you, and you will be in me. I will be your God, and you will be my people. I will be responsible for your healing.

When the Christ comes in, He brings with him everything you will ever need. He brings with him love, joy, peace, and forgiveness for your shortcomings. He brings healing, power, and victory.

ABOUT THE AUTHOR

Dr. Nathea Watts Hutchinson is the proud mother of four children: Stanley E. Watts (deceased), Shannon R. Figueroa, Jonathan B. Hutchinson, and Kaysha S. Hutchinson. She currently resides in Jacksonville, Florida, where she was born and raised. Nathea serves as a leader and mentor for many men, women, and children. Her passion is unlocked through lost and hurting people, people that are stuck in unproductive circumstances and ungodly situations. Her message is "It doesn't have to be that way. You can survive this! God can, and He will, make you free, complete, and whole." Nathea received a doctorate degree in theology from Truth Bible University of Jacksonville.